OYSTER CASE

FLUTED BEZEL

THIS WATCH IS THE EPITOME OF CLASSIC STYLE.

Known for its enduring aesthetics and functions, the Datejust is the archetype of the classic watch. Built the Rolex Way in 1945, it was the world's first self-winding, waterproof wristwatch chronometer to display the date in a window at 3 o'clock on the dial, consolidating all the major innovations that Rolex had brought to the modern wristwatch until then. Emblematic and timeless, the Datejust has spanned eras, while retaining the enduring codes that today still make it one of the world's most recognisable watches. It doesn't just tell time. It tells history.

OYSTER PERPETUAL DATEJUST 41

ROLEX

PARACHUTE

Seize the nap.

PARACHUTEHOME.COM

danish design by · made by

LINDBERG

The Paper Book 2018-2021
Available worldwide in A4 and DL

arjowiggins

International standards
for creative papers

Standards internationaux
pour papiers de création

国际标准的艺术纸

Estándares internacionales
para papeles creativos

2018 –
2021

KINFOLK

FOUNDER & CREATIVE DIRECTOR
Nathan Williams

EDITOR-IN-CHIEF
John Clifford Burns

EDITOR
Harriet Fitch Little

ART DIRECTOR
Christian Møller Andersen

DESIGN DIRECTOR
Alex Hunting

BRAND DIRECTOR
Amy Woodroffe

COPY EDITOR
Rachel Holzman

COMMUNICATIONS DIRECTOR
Jessica Gray

PRODUCER
Cecilie Jegsen

PROJECT MANAGER
Garett Nelson

CASTING DIRECTOR
Sarah Bunter

**SALES & DISTRIBUTION
DIRECTOR**
Frédéric Mähl

**BUSINESS OPERATIONS
MANAGER**
Kasper Schademan

STUDIO MANAGER
Aryana Tajdivand-Echevarria

EDITORIAL ASSISTANTS
Oliver Hugemark
Ulrika Lukševica

CONTRIBUTING EDITORS
Michael Anastassiades
Jonas Bjerre-Poulsen
Andrea Codrington Lippke
Ilse Crawford
Margot Henderson
Leonard Koren
Hans Ulrich Obrist
Amy Sall
Matt Willey

WORDS
Alex Anderson
Ellie Violet Bramley
John Clifford Burns
Katie Calautti
Cody Delistraty
Harriet Fitch Little
Candice Frederick
Nikolaj Hansson
Hugo Macdonald
Sarah Moroz
Justin Myers
John Ovans
Debika Ray
Asher Ross
Tristan Rutherford
Neda Semnani
Charles Shafaieh
Ben Shattuck
Suzanne Snider
Pip Usher
Molly Young

CROSSWORD
Molly Young

PUBLICATION DESIGN
Alex Hunting Studio

STYLING, HAIR & MAKEUP
Rebecca Chang
Ashleigh Ciucci
Cobalto Studio
Liz Daxauer
Taan Doan
Lianna Fowler
Paul Frederick
Andreas Frienholt
Céline Gaulhiac
Lucy Gibson
Cyril Laine
David Nolan
Sandy Suffield
Camille-Joséphine Teisseire

PHOTOGRAPHY
Gustav Almestål
Ian Berry
Luc Braquet
Jessica Brilli
Rala Choi
Nicholas Alan Cope
Pelle Crépin
Jerome De Perlinghi
Bogdan Dreava
Christopher Ferguson
Lasse Fløde
Jean-Marie Franceschi
Alex Freund
François Halard
Adam Katz Sinding
Saul Leiter
Salva López
Christian Møller Andersen
Jacopo Moschin
Justin Poulsen
Dan Smith
Bachar Srour
Aaron Tilley
Zoltan Tombor
Dominique Vellay
Dennis Weber

ISSUE 30

info@kinfolk.com
www.kinfolk.com

Published by Ouur Media
Amagertorv 14, Level 1
1160 Copenhagen, Denmark

The views expressed in Kinfolk magazine are those of the respective contributors and are not necessarily shared by the company or its staff.

SUBSCRIBE
Kinfolk is published four times a year. To subscribe, visit *kinfolk.com/subscribe* or email us at *info@kinfolk.com*

CONTACT US
If you have questions or comments, please write to us at *info@kinfolk.com*. For advertising inquiries, get in touch at *advertising@kinfolk.com*

sleepwear for the modern woman

LUNYA

lunya.co

Welcome

When we invite loved ones over for dinner, we are offering more than nutrition. The good host provides mental sustenance too, feeding the soul as much as the stomach. When M. F. K. Fisher wrote *The Gastronomical Me* in the 1940s, she considered how "our three basic needs, for food and security and love, are so mixed and mingled and entwined that we cannot straightly think of one without the others."

This issue of *Kinfolk* expands on the same psychological entanglement of food and mood to explore hospitality as a conduit for belonging, comfort, empathy, entertainment and trust. These five values are the pillars of good hospitality on any occasion, transforming Airbnb rentals into home-away-from-home experiences and quick suppers with friends into short bursts of therapy. Without the addition of such ingredients, chef Flynn McGarry warns us on page 114, the atmosphere of even the most extravagant evening feels cold: "A fast-food restaurant is similar to a fine-dining restaurant—everything has been meticulously figured out with no room for expression," he says.

We also consider the role society plays as host. "Hospitality suggests a generosity of spirit and a full-throated welcome," writes Neda Semnani on page 176, as she charts the depreciation of *xenia*—the convivial relationship between host and guest—and the rise of its antithetical ideology, xenophobia, spread by the nationalist political parties making electoral gains around the world. Writer Hugo Macdonald considers the role of government in making our cities more hospitable, mapping out the decline of public space on page 138.

At the heart of all hospitality is a sense of community, a theme we continue to explore elsewhere in the issue.

Actress Teyonah Parris speaks of the strength she has found in sisterhood at several critical points in her life, and the duty she feels to reciprocate through the roles she chooses—most recently, in Barry Jenkins' adaptation of the James Baldwin novel *If Beale Street Could Talk*. The poet Eileen Myles explains why they see their peers within the poetry scene as integral to their personal and professional development, and we visit the owners of a French château, for whom the ongoing renovation of their fantasy home would not be possible without a generous band of volunteers.

For winter, we also explore community in chillier scenarios: in the way it haunts our homecomings, in the group huddles that make ghost stories appear exciting rather than terrifying and, hypothetically, in apocalyptic underground bunkers.

JOHN CLIFFORD BURNS

"The house was a place of friendship and open to everyone."
DOMINIQUE VELLAY – P. 80

håndværk

A specialist label creating *luxury basics*.
Ethically crafted with an unwavering
commitment to *exceptional quality*.

handvaerk.com

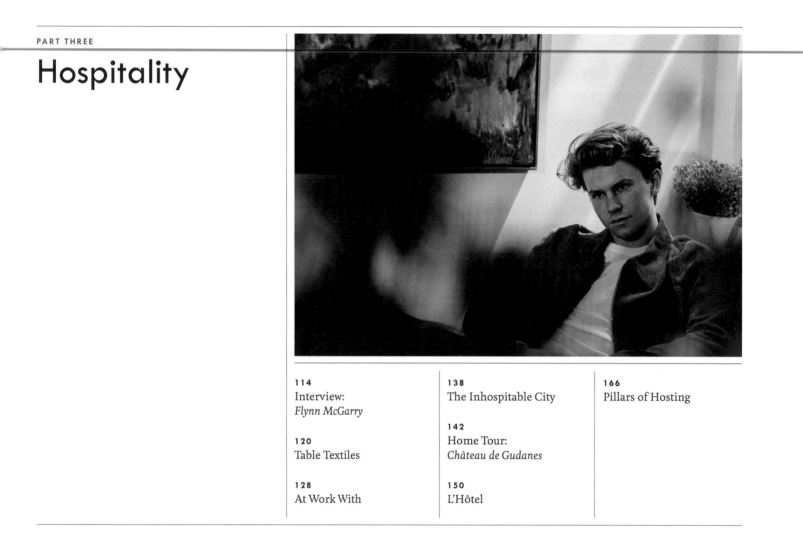
"There's something more emotional about food when your approach is somewhat unhinged."
FLYNN MCGARRY — P. 114

Photography: Jacopo Moschin

RAINS

Drip, drip, drip.

rains.com

MUUTO

1
Starters

ALEX ANDERSON

No Shame

How to refuse humiliation.

The strange pronouncement "shame on you!" hints at the oppressive character of shame—a deeply internalized emotion imposed by others. Shame *on you*. Unlike guilt, shame publicly stigmatizes individuals rather than actions. It assails self-worth, using emotional pain to punish nonconformity. Psychologist Patricia DeYoung describes it as "the enemy of well-being."

There is a barbarism to public humiliation that seems to belong to an age of pillories and dunce caps. But Jon Ronson, in *So You've Been Publicly Shamed*, chronicles "a great renaissance of public shaming" in this century. Fueled by angry politics and a brutal online peanut gallery, it has burgeoned as the penalty for many perceived transgressions. Sometimes the justification seems irrefutable: #MeToo throws off the victims' shame and places it on its proper recipients. When laws don't deter and punish perpetrators, ignominy diminishes them. Often, though, gleeful haranguers cast shame for lifestyles (chosen or inherent), impolitic speech, even unattractiveness. The damage can be swift and unjust. It seems reasonable, then, to resist this enemy of well-being. But how?

Literature, often a useful guide, offers some intriguing approaches. In Oscar Wilde's *The Picture of Dorian Gray*, dissimulation does the job, but not very well. Gray avoids public condemnation for social and moral infractions by hiding behind the mask of perpetual youth and beauty, while his portrait absorbs the ugly blots of degeneracy. He finds, however, that brazen shamelessness is no shield against mortification. As his offenses accumulate, Gray descends into self-reproach and tries to mutilate the portrait, the "visible emblem of his conscience." Instead, he destroys himself. It was Dorian Gray's "duty," Wilde writes, "to confess, to suffer public shame and to make public atonement."

In *The Scarlet Letter*, Nathaniel Hawthorne's 19th-century masterwork, Hester Prynne does just that. She admits culpability for adultery and defiantly suffers public shame, but refuses to let it diminish her. She crafts the elaborately embroidered scarlet "A" she wears across her chest (instead of a less conspicuous version the conviction for adultery requires) "with so much fertility and gorgeous luxuriance of fancy" that it becomes an emblem not just of public degradation but also of Prynne's dominance over it. One bitter old Puritan in the jeering crowd gripes that the ornamentation makes "a pride out of" what was "meant for a punishment." Prynne's unabashed demeanor feels equally galling. Her steady gaze boldly deflects shame, turning it back on sanctimonious accusers who carry their own hidden and unpunished transgressions. Over time, Prynne's stoicism gains reluctant admiration—Hawthorne calls it "reverence"—even among her most zealous oppressors. Calculated defiance protects Prynne, while brash dissimulation doesn't help Dorian Gray.

These accounts hint at a strange thing about shame: It isn't very useful. Its most deserving victims—the powerful and blameworthy—find ways to slip out from under it. Meanwhile, the taunting mob diminishes itself in smug self-satisfaction as it gleefully heaps scorn on its victims. Those few who, like Hester Prynne, stand up to its burden and turn it back on the crowd demonstrate the ennobling power of resistance.

Resistance buttresses an idea of innate human worth, irrespective of blame. It strengthens the individual who has been targeted by the catcalling crowd and the vindictive Twitter mob. Resistance starts neither with shamelessness nor calculated disregard; it does not help simply to avoid or ignore the emotion.

"There should be no shame," DeYoung writes, "in acknowledging our shame." This steady-eyed outlook may not appease angry accusers, but it allows for atonement for whatever harm might have been done. It also prompts a turn inward, not in supplication to the horde, but in consideration of one's inherent value, of the fleeting character of past actions, and a mutual condition of human imperfection. This brings with it a realization that there are always quieter counterparts to the shaming throng, others who are more sympathetic to our well-being and those who are willing to accept us as we are.

Ready and Willing

What to do when the world ends.

All humans have an inherent desire to control the unpredictable twists of everyday life. The global (but mainly American) community of "preppers" takes the instinct further: They believe they can ready themselves for the apocalypse. Also known as survivalists, preppers hunker down in remote bunkers and surround themselves with weapons and supplies in the expectation that, come doomsday, society will break down into a Hobbesian state of nature—where life will be solitary, poor, nasty, brutish and short, and it'll be every man (they're usually men) for himself.

The attitude of preppers is merely an extreme version of how we all think about external threats. "We just can't bear the idea that disaster is completely random," says seismologist Lucy Jones, author of the book *The Big Ones*, which explores the history and cultural impact of natural disasters. And in its extremeness, the lifestyle choices of survivalists raise an eternal question about human nature: Are we inherently selfish or instinctively communal? Jones points out that public messaging around disaster preparedness often reinforces an individualistic approach to a crisis: "It tends to be, 'You're going to be on your own, you have to defend your family.' There's a subliminal message that your neighbor may become your enemy and can't be trusted." In fact, she says, high levels of "social capital"—the term sociologists use to quantify interpersonal relationships—is one of the best predictors of recovery from a disaster. Using the impact of Hurricane Katrina in New Orleans as an example, she says: "The best predictor was the neighborhood that put together a Mardi Gras float. All the skills involved—working with neighbors, organizing volunteers—are good for handling an emergency response. Anything that strengthens the community improves your ability to recover."

It's a valuable insight at a time when human-induced climate change is expected to generate more weather-related catastrophes. Whatever our instincts, we can't resist such forces alone. Preppers, if you're listening: Unlock your bunker and invite a neighbor in for Spam and crackers.

LAST ORDERS

by Harriet Fitch Little

In the pandemonium of preparing for the end of days, you might forget to pack a corkscrew. Don't panic (any more than is already necessary). If you have the good fortune to find yourself bunking down in a wine cellar, many of the survival tools in your go-bag will double as makeshift bottle openers. Place two nails in a bottle's cork and then use the claw of a hammer to prise it out. Or put the wine, bottom first, in a shoe—hopefully you fled wearing a sturdy pair—and hit it gently against the wall. Here are some more go-bag essentials that will make you the envy of any zombie with half a brain. (Top: Matchbox by HAY. Center: Whistle from Labour And Wait. Bottom: Keyring by COS.)

Left Photograph: Nicholas Alan Cope. Right Photographs: Christian Møller Andersen (Top, Middle), Courtesy of COS (Bottom).

Can passwords unlock personalities?

JOHN OVANS

Codes of Behavior

Photograph: Bogdan Dreava

Passwords are often deeply personal. In one episode of the BBC drama *Sherlock*, Holmes correctly guesses that the combination to his romantic interest's safe are her body measurements.

What do the words "dragon," "baseball" and "pussy" have in common? They all regularly appear on lists of the most commonly used computer passwords. They make the grade year after year because dragons, baseball and pussies (meaning cats, of course) are all things that people like. Human sentimentality is the enemy of internet security, which makes banks' obsession with knowing our first pets' names and the streets we grew up on seem counterintuitive; these are words that stick in our mind, but they are not reliable gatekeepers.

In a study of the psychology of password selection, Helen Petrie, professor of human-computer interaction at the University of York, undertook a survey of 1,200 British computer users and established four main password personality classifications: family-oriented (words connected with family, partner or pet); fans (the names of celebrities, athletes other idols); fantasists ("sexy," "stud") and finally cryptics, who opt for a random string of numbers, letters and symbols. Only 10 percent of those surveyed were classed as cryptics because it turns out that most of us opt for convenience over actual security—and something is more convenient when it carries enough emotional resonance that it can be easily remembered. "People take a nonnatural requirement imposed on them, like memorizing a password, and make it a meaningful human experience," computer scientist Joseph Bonneau told *The New York Times* in 2014 when the paper published an article on password selection. It included anecdotal examples ranging from a man who successfully used motivational mantras to help him achieve personal goals (quit@smoking4ever) to a runner with the password 16:59—her target time in the 5,000-meter track event. The average computer user regularly accesses 28 online accounts. Given the increasingly frequent imperative to add numbers, symbols and uppercase letters, are we fast approaching a future where we all have to simply embrace being cryptics? Security's gain would be a human loss; many of us use passwords as an opportunity to articulate something truly private, perhaps something that might never have been uttered otherwise. A truly impenetrable password reveals nothing of the mind of its creator.

Filippa Knutsson

The Filippa K founder on how minimalism grew up.

Photograph: Dan Smith

Along with its secondhand store, Filippa K has started a scheme that allows people to borrow clothes rather than buy them—an effort to cut down on the waste of fast fashion.

When Swedish designer Filippa Knutsson launched her eponymous label 25 years ago, "Scandinavian minimalism" was simply a way of describing a place and a style—not shorthand for a global aesthetic. Now, the stars have aligned for Filippa K: Its aesthetic, one of stripped-back luxury, is perennially in fashion, and its ethos of sustainability is in the ascendant. From her home in North London, Knutsson—who recently returned to the helm after five years away from the company she founded—talks to *Harriet Fitch Little* about how her designs still jump off the rails after a quarter century, and the importance of a little bit of bad taste.

You founded Filippa K in the early 1990s. What made it the right moment to launch a minimalist clothing line? It was a reaction to the '80s, which in fashion was a period with a lot of decoration, a lot of maximalism. I had this longing for something very pure, simple and minimal—and for more of a capsule wardrobe philosophy.

How has the landscape changed 25 years later? In the 1990s, minimalism was an aesthetic movement, whereas today it's more of a conscious choice based on questions of sustainability. Overconsuming just doesn't feel very modern anymore—it almost feels irresponsible. I have a daughter who works at Filippa K and she's part of a generation that doesn't understand why you would consume more clothes than necessary. There's a new renaissance in really looking at the basics.

You've described minimalism as "the purest form of luxury." How so? Filippa K is the antithesis of what a lot of people associate with luxury today, but that process of stripping things back and just leaving the core is what ultimate luxury is for me. Quality is incredibly important if you want to go for that "sophisticated simplicity" look. For simple clothes to not be boring, fit becomes very important—the choices you make all matter more.

Filippa K has firm roots in Scandinavian style, but you are based in London. What do you gain from living in the UK? I lived in Paris for three years and people are much more inspiring style-wise there. But London to me is more inspiring in terms of its energy—open, nonjudgmental and super international.

What's the oldest item in your wardrobe? I've got jersey tunics and sloppy pants that are 10 years old and still look good, and a seven-year-old tuxedo jacket that I wear. That's one of the main ways in which our clothing is sustainable; it's well-made and in long-lasting styles. Very early on, we launched a Filippa K secondhand store in Stockholm which is still going strong. Going there is amazing. I'm always thinking, "Oh my God, I remember that. It's still really good!"

Is there anything about the way you dress that would surprise devotees of your label? I'm not some rigid minimalist. Especially in the summertime, I wear a lot of colors. Diana Vreeland said something like, "We all need a splash of bad taste." I think Italians have a great sense of how to do that. I certainly don't believe Filippa K should provide everything a woman needs ever, but we can provide a good platform to build a stylishly functional wardrobe around.

"Minimalism is a conscious choice. Overconsuming just doesn't feel very modern."

KNOWING ME, KNOWING YOU
by Harriet Fitch Little

The odds of a person encountering their doppelgänger are narrowing. Facial recognition software and the internet have made the identification of "double walkers" (from the German) into a pastime open to all amateur sleuths. But the thrill we feel today on spotting our likeness in others is a historic anomaly: Doppelgängers are more often associated with death than with pleasant diversion. A slew of legends from across cultures cast them as paranormal duplicates and as phantoms to be avoided at all costs. From Queen Elizabeth I and Catherine the Great to the poet Percy Shelley—whose relatives claim he was greeted one night, shortly before his death, by a doppelgänger who asked him, "How long do you mean to be content?"—the apparition of a double has gone down in history as a warning that the end of life is near. In some cases, there may indeed be a scientific link between these encounters and the threat of death: Neuropsychologist Peter Brugger documented the case of a man who attempted suicide after seeing "himself" lying on his bed (a hallucination that doctors later discovered was caused by a tumor on his left frontal lobe). But science also gives us cause to relax our superstitions. According to researchers at the University of Adelaide, the chances of encountering someone who genuinely looks like you are in excess of a trillion to one. *Photography by Adam Katz Sinding*

Janou Pakter
& Damian Chiam

A discussion about the nature of talent.

Having a career we love is generally considered one path to a fulfilling life. However, aspiring to a job we're actually good at can be an equally meaningful—and more realistic—vision. But how do we know where our talents lie, let alone which jobs might value them? After four years of collaboration at Janou LLC—a global executive search firm specializing in creative and marketing fields—Janou Pakter and Damian Chiam have honed their ability to pinpoint talent and precision-calibrate it into a professional fit. Here, the duo—or "the odd couple" as Pakter likes to joke—offers advice on how to identify and nurture creative talent and standing out from the crowd.

Social media has made many of us experts in the art of self-promotion. What does true talent look like? Pakter: Talent means original thinking. There are many designers or art directors whose work you will look at and think is beautiful, but true talent is when you're different and original and the concept is really yours. True talent is not one-dimensional. It has a holistic vision and sees possibilities between existing models and new technology.

Chiam: To me, talent has a very human aspect—the curiosity to see the beauty in the ordinary. We try to distinguish ourselves in how we work with the talent. It's more than a transaction, we care about the person and their story and their journey.

Is talent innate or can it be learned? Pakter: Some people are amazingly wacky and talented and they hone those qualities to get better. But, if you have the passion and desire then you can—with training, education and hard work—excel as much as, if not more than, the people who are born with it. You need the drive. You need to be able to start and finish. A lot of people, no matter how brilliant they are, don't always finish.

What do you most admire in each other? Pakter: Damian quit a full-time job to come and join as my partner. That shows an incredible amount of courage and vision. It's something I will never forget. On a more practical note, Damian is thorough and exact, and together we have achieved incredible success.

Chiam: Clients and candidates consistently speak highly of Janou, highlighting her industry knowledge, integrity and kindness. As her partner, I'm very respectful of that. I think it's amazing that Janou is changing people's lives by using her intuition and connection with people to further their career.

Is there an element of matchmaking to your work? Pakter: We rely a great deal on our intuition. Because we understand our client's needs and culture so well, we know right away which candidates are going to be a great match. We've made a lot of placements like that without being too literal and primarily looking at education, years in industry and experience.

Chiam: It's about connecting and understanding interests. We want to get a good overall picture of them and where they're at in life. It's quite a close relationship—almost like buying a home—because, as a candidate, you're sharing quite a bit about your personal life. It's really about getting to know people and what motivates them.

What's your advice for people hoping to get noticed for their creativity? Pakter: Clients are looking for a Renaissance-type person with both left and right brain thinking. If you can only come up with creative ideas, then you're not going to be of any value unless you can bring that within the spectrum of what is good for the brand. That's a different kind of profile than in the past. It's become much broader, deeper and more integrated. The other thing that's important is a sense of integrity and authenticity. Brands are interested in people who are into sustainability, empathy, a better earth. So if these passions are important to you, you should express that creatively in your work.
—

This feature was produced in partnership with Janou LLC

BEN SHATTUCK

On Homecoming

There's no place like home—and no returning to it.

A hometown is a place left behind. There are the famous ones: the Garden of Eden, Ithaca, the Shire, Mark Twain's Hannibal. Those who have moved away carry with them stories of how good it used to be, and of how they can't go back—not really. Sometimes the place is gone (Eden, for example), but more often, the traveler has changed too much (Odysseus, Frodo, Twain), wedged in too much living, so even in return the place feels distant. What's left is the rosy past: the old house, the friend knocking on your door after school, the ice-cream truck's song coming down the street. It's the way things used to be, whatever that was. "Always it comes when we least expect it, like a wave," Midwestern bard and Pulitzer Prize winner Charles Wright wrote of nostalgia. "Or like the shadow of several waves, one after the

Artwork: Nebraska by Jessica Brilli

next, becoming singular as the face of someone who rose and fell apart at the edge of our lives."

In centuries past, your hometown was just your town. When William the Conqueror invaded England in 1066, most English men and women were born, lived and died within a few square miles. The compound word "hometown" doesn't even appear in English writing until the mid-1800s, when Americans started hoofing cross-country, followed quickly thereafter by literature about the ache of leaving. Migration has only increased: Today, Americans move about 11 times in a lifetime, and most don't live where they grew up. Everyone has a hometown buried in their past, and likely everyone misses it, in some way, even if they hate it.

As Annie Dillard wrote of Pittsburgh, a hometown is where "the

mystery of existence" first beats down. It is the stage where you act out an early notion of the self—the one who walks with you through your life and who in some way yearns to be brought back. You might love your hometown, memorializing its mountains and alpine lakes (Marilynne Robinson, Idaho) or hay fields (Wendell Berry, Kentucky), but most people have complicated relationships with them; they are simultaneously repelled by and attracted to it. Antiguan-American writer Jamaica Kincaid wrote of her hometown, "It is as if, then, the beauty—the beauty of the sea, the land, the air, the trees, the market, the people, the sounds they make—were a prison, and as if everything and everybody inside it were locked in and everything and everybody that is not inside it were locked out." If you do return,

the good memories will likely be destroyed by the requirements of adulthood; Ithaca was surely not the same for Odysseus after he butchered all those suitors. Even if your homecoming doesn't involve finding your wife surrounded by a hundred men that need offing, you might find the Dairy Queen gone—and with it that sense of childhood wonder.

"There is no there there," Gertrude Stein woefully wrote of her return to Oakland, California. After distancing herself first by a country's length, and then by an ocean and another language, she found the rural acres of orchards in California where she had grown up replaced by housing developments. All she had left were memories of wandering through the sweet-smelling fields and lying in the grass with the sun, of chopping wood, making hay and listening to

the wind. And so she, like many others, rebuilt it somewhere else—in writing. Nostalgia is too great a destroyer of the present to be given breathing room. The truth is, it probably wasn't better back in the day. And even if it was, who cares? In his most recent novel, *Lincoln in the Bardo*, George Saunders wrote about the toxic gravity of nostalgia, in a way. Ghosts who obsess about returning to their "hometowns"—the land of the living—linger in the graveyard where the novel is set. If they let go of their pasts they'll be freed from the cemetery, able to pass into the afterlife. Instead, they remain in purgatory, maimed by memories.

Better to heed Charles Wright's plea about hometown sentimentality at the end of his poem, "Nostalgia": "May it never arrive," he writes of its nomenclature. "Lord, may it never arrive."

Dorval collection by SCMP DESIGN OFFICE
Edited by Lambert & Fils

lambert&fils

JOHN CLIFFORD BURNS

Hamed Sinno

From the Beirut underground to the world stage.

Hamed Sinno is the lead singer and lyricist of Mashrou' Leila—the Beirut-based quintet that has crowdfunded its way to being the biggest indie pop band in the Arab world. Although Sinno says he has been known to spend weeks "on the couch binge-watching horrible television with the sole purpose of avoiding dealing with life," Mashrou' Leila's music very much suggests that he spends most of his time doing the opposite. Lyrics—sung in Arabic—on the band's latest album, *Ibn El Leil*, reference Sylvia Plath, Allen Ginsberg, Abu Nawas and Sappho, and most definitely confront life's iniquities: from homophobia and political oppression to misogyny and toxic masculinity.

Where do you write most of your songs? Planes, trains or any other space that I can't exit but still feel like I'm moving in. Mind-set is a bit trickier; I wish I knew what

inspires me. That would make my life so much easier. I find happiness incredibly unremarkable, despite its rarity, so I seldom write about anything that feels obviously pleasant.

Writing lyrics is a deeply personal endeavor. How does it feel when they resonate with others? Having so many people relate to my writing makes me feel like perhaps my sentiments aren't that anomalous. In some ways, it makes me feel pleasantly basic. On the other hand, writing is as much about the reader as it is about the writer. A couple of years ago, we were touring the USA and had written "Maghawir"—a song about toxic masculinity and club shootings, mostly inspired by a couple of incidents that happened in Lebanon. Then, [the mass shooting at the Pulse nightclub in] Orlando happened. Because of our history of dealing with both queer and

Muslim representation, we suddenly found ourselves in this really strange position: The press was almost asking us to weigh in at a time when those two communities were being pitted against each other. It was completely surreal to see that track transform in the public eye as audiences began injecting their own readings.

Visibility is hugely important, but can being a poster boy ever endanger your own personal development? I made my peace with that a while ago. I sort of just decided that my life, and my decisions, would always have to be about me and me alone. I never set out to "represent" anyone other than myself. When that resonates with people, it feels amazing and so rewarding, but that's where it ends. It would be impossible to write—or do anything else for that matter—while thinking about other people and their expectations.

DEBIKA RAY

On Nudging

A lesson in pushing without shoving.

Why are we so uncomfortable with the idea of being manipulated when we do it to others all the time? When you smile in a job interview, you're trying to make the interviewer warm to you. When you go on a date, you think about the location, the ambiance, the food and wine—all in an effort to exert influence. Doctors and shopkeepers alike offer options with the intention of pushing people to make certain choices.

You might refer to these behaviors as "nudges": subtle modifications in the presentation of a set of options that affect a person's automatic, rather than rational, cognitive processes. In recent years, even governments have seized on the tactic. In 2010, inspired by Nobel Prize-winning economist Richard Thaler, and the book he co-authored, *Nudge: Improving Decisions About Health, Wealth, and Happiness*, the British government set up its Behavioural Insights Team to apply these theories to public policy. Several similar "nudge units" have been set up around the world since then. The proposals that emerge from such organizations include placing healthier foods at eye level in school cafeterias and making employees opt out of, rather than opt in to, workplace pension plans.

Their emergence has sparked ethical concerns. When we enter a supermarket, we know it's trying to profit from our presence and are confident we can resist, say, the candy placed by the checkout counter. But the idea that a government may be covertly manipulating our choices troubles us more than blunter instruments such as taxes and regulations because it implies that we don't have free will.

It need not be this way, says Pelle Guldborg Hansen, a behavioral scientist at Denmark's Roskilde University and a founder of the European Nudge Network and consultancy iNudgeYou. "You can nudge people while still respecting their autonomy," he says. He distinguishes between transparent and non-transparent nudges—with the former, you know you're being influenced, by whom, and why. "If you send a text to remind people to go to the dentist, they start showing up, but only if they want to go—if they're afraid, it won't work," Hansen says. He adds that transparent nudges can also be more effective in cases where they remind people of their long-term goals—the principle behind fitness trackers and real-time banking apps. Of course, transparency is no good if you're trying to push people to do things they disagree with—but there's clearly something undemocratic about removing the option to rebel.

When it comes to your private life, it's reasonable to apply the same standards. Take that date, for example—you may engage in a ritual of subtle, short-term influence, but eventually, you want your partner to commit freely. "Ultimately," Hansen says, "respecting people's autonomy is a long-term strategy that works."

Restaurants use nudge theory to encourage customers to up their spend; the inclusion of one very expensive wine on a menu leads to more people buying the second priciest bottle.

Photograph: Aaron Tilley, Set Design: Sandy Suffield

Photograph: Alex Freund / The Licensing Project

CHARLES SHAFAIEH

Cold Shivers

"Whenever five or six English-speaking people meet round a fire on Christmas Eve, they start telling each other ghost stories," wrote Jerome K. Jerome in his 1891 story collection, *Told After Supper*. This custom, heightened during the macabre-embracing Victorian era, may have its origins in the Yuletide season's pagan antecedents: At the darkest point of the year, the boundary between the living and the dead is believed to be thinnest, conjuring weirdness, worry and unease.

Like all folklore, ghost stories serve educative purposes. Mexican children, for example, are taught to avoid wandering alone late at night for fear of La Llorona—a woman believed to haunt riverbanks looking for her drowned children. They can also reveal uncomfortable truths: In the United States, the panoply of stories featuring Native American ghosts suggests the unresolved trauma and guilt concerning the colonization of indigenous people's lands.

Such cautionary and ethical elements do not, however, reveal what attracts us to ghost stories. They are, in their way, tragedies, and therefore cathartic—we purge feelings of fear through engaging with them. Or as H. P. Lovecraft posited in relation to the genre of horror, certain stories conjure a fear different from that instinct which causes us to flee dangerous situations. "Cosmic horror," as he termed it, creates a kind of awe; it attracts us not through gore or shock, but by validating the notion that unknown forces exist in the world. We tell ghost stories in groups because there is comfort in numbers for those afraid, and yet we have been telling them less and less. In his 1911 essay *The Storyteller*, German philosopher Walter Benjamin suggests that storytelling, once integral to many societies, is disappearing. A century on, his observation has been confirmed. In a sense, all storytelling has become haunted by the ghosts of times gone by.

The seasonal appeal of ghost stories.

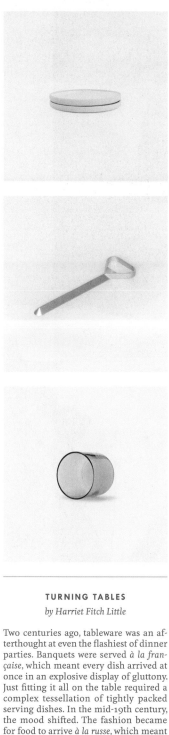

Left Photographs: Courtesy of Frama (Top), Christian Møller Andersen (Middle), Courtesy of WallpaperSTORE* (Bottom). Right Photograph: Gustav Almestål

TURNING TABLES
by Harriet Fitch Little

Two centuries ago, tableware was an afterthought at even the flashiest of dinner parties. Banquets were served *à la française*, which meant every dish arrived at once in an explosive display of gluttony. Just fitting it all on the table required a complex tessellation of tightly packed serving dishes. In the mid-19th century, the mood shifted. The fashion became for food to arrive *à la russe*, which meant one course at a time. The table, no longer creaking under the weight of a banquet, suddenly looked very bare. Introducing different glasses and silverware for every course (of which there were often more than a dozen) was a way to fill the gaps—and show off. (Top: Otto plates by Frama. Center: Bottle opener by HAY. Bottom: Glassware by Eligo.)

ASHER ROSS

Strange Voices

Why do we hate the way we sound?

Almost nobody likes their voice when they hear it on a recording. The sound is weaker, shriller, more obnoxious than we'd like—an unbearable parody of something deeply personal. All our lives we've heard our voice as it resonates while speaking. And now we're confronted with incontrovertible evidence that everyone we've ever spoken to has been hearing something so much... worse!

What accounts for the difference? Dr. Tyler Perrachione, of Boston University's Department of Speech, Language and Hearing Sciences, has some insight. "When we hear our own voice, the sound reaches our ears both through the air around us and through our own head," he says. "Because the head is denser than air, it emphasizes the low frequencies in sound, so we get used to hearing our voice sounding deeper and more resonant than it sounds only through the air. When we hear our voice on a recording, the sound is coming only through the air. This makes our voice sound very different —higher, squeakier, less mellow." Perrachione explains why we find that unpleasant: "In part, it's because culturally we tend to ascribe attractive features to voices that are lower and more mellow, and less attractive features to voices that are higher and squeakier. When you hear your own voice with fewer low frequencies, you sound less attractive than you expect."

But mechanics can only partially explain why it is so cringeworthy to hear our voice played back. Perrachione observes that a big part of the problem is psychological. "When we sound differently than we expect to it's surprising, and surprises can be upsetting, especially when they throw into doubt something affecting our identity, like the sound of our voice." A scientist's understatement to be sure. Our connection with our own voice has roots in our earliest memories. In moments of crisis, human beings talk to themselves, as if to keep track of who they are. Through our tears, we hear our voice fastening on painful truths and phantoms. We've heard it whispering secrets to children and to spouses. It's not just the timbre of our voice that counts; our accent helps tell the story of where we have lived and, like a palimpsest, contains the echoes of our mothers, fathers and loved ones. There is a logic to the expression that a successful artist is said to have "found their voice"; in its infinite variety, voice is the great musician of the self. Such a shame that nobody else can hear it quite right.

STARTERS

Every stranger has a story.

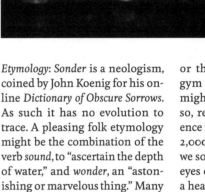

ASHER ROSS

Word: Sonder

R&B singer Brent Faiyaz called his
popular debut album *Sonder Son*—
a reference to the awareness of being
one of the many people trying to
"make it" in Los Angeles.

Etymology: *Sonder* is a neologism,
coined by John Koenig for his online *Dictionary of Obscure Sorrows*.
As such it has no evolution to
trace. A pleasing folk etymology
might be the combination of the
verb *sound*, to "ascertain the depth
of water," and *wonder*, an "aston-
ishing or marvelous thing." Many
alternatives have been proposed
by the dictionary's devotees.

Meaning: Koenig's definition
begins: "The realization that each
random passerby is living a life as
vivid and complex as your own,"
and expands into a brief but beautiful prose poem, like many en-
tries in his dictionary. He likes to
say that sonder is the revelation
that you are merely an extra in
someone else's story.

Sonder shouldn't be confused
with empathy. Nor is it meant to
convey a psychological theory of
the mind—the working understanding that allows us to attribute
feelings, thoughts and motivations
to others. Sonder is a far rarer bird.
Like *déjà vu* it takes hold of us un-
bidden; it's a sublime experience
that is perhaps too intense to be
part of everyday cognition. In order to feel it, we must first ascend
to an almost out-of-body state.

The woman staring into space
at the grocery store might be experiencing a moment of sonder,
or the teenager pausing at his
gym locker. The concert cellist
might feel it once every year or
so, remembering that her audience is not a pointillistic mass, but
2,000 strangers adrift. In sonder
we sound the depths of the world,
eyes open or closed, attaining for
a heartbeat a god's-eye view.

And what fine acrobatics the
ego performs! Fleeing itself in order to make room, unfurling like a
screen on which shadows are cast.
Sonder teaches us not to diminish the complexity of another person's experience because it is unlike our own, and how—by twists
and turns—we become just one
mind among many. When in its
throes, we can feel the roots that
bind us to all others.

No wonder the newly-minted
word has captured the popular
imagination, becoming the name
of—among other things—a start-
up brewery, an Airbnb competitor
and an Australian theatre troupe.
It resonates with any endeavor
that aims to gather people.

We can never know another
person completely, far less a billion people. We can't taste wine
as they taste it, nor hear music
through their ears. And yet—how
close we are to each other in these
rare moments of sonder and how
luminous the world becomes.

Akwaeke Emezi

An interview with the author who finished writing three novels before her first was even published.

Photography: Jacopo Moschin

Akwaeke Emezi's social media followers love the videos she posts of herself dancing when she's in a particularly good mood—and, lately, she has had many reasons to celebrate. The Igbo and Tamil writer's debut novel, *Freshwater*, was published to resounding praise in early 2018, prompting the sale of two future novels. Both the protagonist of her unflinching bildungsroman and the author herself identify as *ogbanje*—in Emezi's words, "an Igbo spirit that's born into a human body, a kind of malevolent trickster whose goal is to torment the human mother by dying unexpectedly only to return in the next child and do it all over again." Wresting Igbo spiritualism from colonial interpretations that see it as a relic of the past, *Freshwater* situates that spirituality in a contemporary context. The book also challenges popular conceptions of female and queer identity and the self in general. It is as uncompromising as Emezi herself.

Before deciding to write full-time in 2014, you attended veterinarian school for two years. What did you learn there that has stayed with you? I learned a lot about how I learn. I was very good at taking tests and retaining knowledge temporarily—which isn't useful if you're in the medical field! Anatomy, for example, was easy for me because it required a lot of memorizing, but other courses weren't. I called my dad the second time I failed physiochemistry and was terrified to tell him because I remember the first B grade I ever got, when I was nine, which made him furious. But he laughed at me instead and told me I'd never had to really work at anything, that I had always coasted, and now I would have to learn what it was like to try.

One of my professors—a cranky old man who nobody liked but me, because I grew up in a culture in which rigor was a way of showing care—eventually gave me permission to just *stop*, which no one had ever really done before. So I left and went to New York to get a master's in public administration, because the only way I could placate my family was by getting a graduate degree.

Were you writing that entire time? Yes, I've been writing since I was 5. My mom has these little books that I wrote and illustrated when I was 7, one of which has a third-person bio that says, "Her ambition is to become a world-famous artist and writer." When I stopped working in a nonprofit where I ran a resource website and started writing full-time, my mom sent that to me. I thought my parents were going to push back more than they did, but they weren't that surprised; I'd been writing for so long, it was kind of inevitable.

Your master's degree brought you to New York, where you've stayed ever since. Do you consider it home now? I consider it *a* home. I tried finding somewhere else, though. I don't have a lot of career goals, but one of them is to get a bungalow. I grew up in one, and there's a particular feel to it that I like: a yard, fruit trees, painted colors. So I went traveling to find out where I might want it. I was living in Trinidad for a while and then was in Nigeria, Singapore, Malaysia, Tanzania… but after all of it, I got tired and realized that adjusting to a new city is really hard—especially when it's in a different country. I hadn't moved countries since I was 16. So I came back to Brooklyn, because I wanted to be in a place that felt familiar, and that's when I realized that Brooklyn is one of my homes. It's also the only place in America where I've lived just to live, not just for school. In that sense, there's a hometown feel to it.

How do you find the solitude here that you've said you need in order to write? I tend not to leave my apartment. When people tell me they find New York very exhausting, I tell them it's because they have a social life—which will do that to you. If you just avoid that, everything's fine! My home is quiet, and I write better there. I'm not one of those people who likes to write in cafés because that means

"*I grew up in a culture in which rigor was a way of showing care.*"

Emezi's debut novel *Freshwater* is heavily autobiographical, and wrestles with the limitations of existing in a single body.

you have to change out of your pajamas and pay for snacks. I try to make sure that wherever I'm living feels like a sanctuary, where all the noisy parts outside disappear. Most of my friends had no idea where I lived in my last apartment here, and even now very few people come into my home. I feel very strongly about bubbles and maintaining them, being rigorous about the boundaries that demarcate them and what passes in and out.

Do you balance that solitude, in a way, with your active presence on social media? I've been thinking recently about how manipulated and curated that social media self is. I often talk with my sister

Yagazie, a photographer who has a much larger following than I do, about how people think they know you because your digital persona seems very accessible, but they don't differentiate between that persona and the actual person. For example, one reader review of *Freshwater* expressed disappointment because they expected the book to be like my Instagram profile, which is more light and positive. Some people think everything you make will be a manifestation of your true self, and that my true self is my Instagram profile.

When the novel came out, I wasn't just who I'd been online but now also "an author" who would

be doing readings and events, and people who knew me only on social media were going to meet me in person. My digital self used to be just another version of me and I could talk more freely, but now it's my professional self. Whatever I put online is going to be seen by editors and critics. It took me most of 2018 to adjust and surrender to that, because there's nothing I could do about it.

Has your recent success made you more cautious about what you share? I've had to find a balance. I worried that how I was on Instagram would be seen as unprofessional and that there would be consequences for it—reper-

cussions happening in rooms I wasn't even in. But I decided not to pull back because I don't believe in being controlled by fear. I spent a large part of my life doing that, and *not* doing that is a very costly freedom that I'm not inclined to give up.

I've had to choose to allow the fear, yes, but still do the things I want to do anyway. It might affect my career in the future—I don't know anyone who's won a MacArthur Fellowship who has a video of them dancing in a bikini online—but the real decision I made was being myself and understanding that this choice may cost me things, even things I might never find out about.

2
Features

Tey

What does it take to get on *Barry Jenkins'* call sheet? *Candice Frederick* speaks to the woman who knows.

Photography by *Jacopo Moschin* & Styling by *Paul Frederick*

ona

h

"Divine destiny" is the phrase that first comes to mind when considering Teyonah Parris' career. The 31-year-old actress has made her way up from trying her luck as a "ham" in beauty pageants in her native South Carolina to being sought out by some of the biggest power players in Hollywood.

But to call it destiny would be to undermine Parris' own talent and tenacity: It's a combination of hard work blended with a Juilliard education and a supportive black sisterhood that has led her to groundbreaking acting roles in the films *Dear White People*, *Chi-Raq* and *If Beale Street Could Talk* and, on the small screen, in *Mad Men*, *Survivor's Remorse* and *Empire*.

Parris recalls that her flair for captivating an audience came to her suddenly. She was a young girl growing up in Hopkins, South Carolina, climbing trees and running around. "We didn't have social media like we do now," Parris remembers. "It was really just me and my brothers and my grandparents and my friends. I think having that sort of freedom [forces] you to be creative in order to have fun." Without fully knowing where her gift lay, only that she was destined to do something that involved her imagination, she enrolled at the South Carolina Governor's School for the Arts

and Humanities. She blossomed. "Going to the Governor's School took that freedom, that instinct, that spontaneity and helped me to actually learn the craft of acting," she says. "Before, it was just a hobby and something fun to do, which it still is. But being able to gain the tools and techniques to sustain what I naturally had was helpful."

If she had to pinpoint her "aha" moment, it would be in 2002 when she watched Halle Berry accept the Academy Award for best actress—the first and only for a black woman. "That's when it changed for me," she recalls. "I was sitting there watching her on TV and was so inspired by [how big] this moment was for the entire world. [I thought] 'I could do that. I want to inspire people and have young girls like me look up to me and say, "Wow, she made history. She told stories. She affected our lives and inspired me to follow my dreams."'"

Parris still reflects on this moment today when she thinks about the impact she wants to make as an actress. When you consider the roles she's played—the determined college student defining blackness on her own terms (*Dear White People*), the modern-day black queen taking control of her body and sexuality (*Chi-Raq*) or the black secretary confronting

Previous spread and right: Parris wears a coat by The Row. Left: She wears a sweater by Helmut Lang.

white supremacy (*Mad Men*)—it seems she is making her message clear. "Certainly, with every role, I ask what the character has to say. How does she add to the narrative of being a human, but more specifically a woman and a black woman?" says Parris. "No matter what I do and what roles I choose, I'm going to be a black woman."

Despite being a part of an industry that undeniably favors white actors, she's never felt isolated in the struggle. In fact, she recalls the sense of camaraderie she experienced among the other budding black actresses while a student at the Juilliard School in New York. It's a feeling she holds dear today; the same classmates—Danielle Brooks, Samira Wiley and Nicole Beharie—remain her peers and sisters. She is also grateful to the black female alumni, like Tracie Thoms and Rutina Wesley, who would come back and offer warm support. "They were huge supporters who had already gone through the program and let us know that we weren't alone. I'm still extremely close with the people I came out of there with. I learned so much about myself [at Juilliard] because I was deconstructed and forced to look at pieces of myself to figure out what is it I'm made of. What is it that I hide? What are the things that I've allowed others to tell me about who I am—but may not be who I am? These women went on that journey with me."

This journey toward feeling comfortable in herself was not strictly limited to her time at the prestigious arts school. It's something she's continued in the years that have followed. For example, after years of relaxing her hair, she realized one day that she had "no clue" what her natural hair looked like. Making the decision to go natural required "a re-conditioning of my mind of what I thought beauty was... I didn't associate how I looked in my natural state with beauty," she says. "And I had to change that for myself." Now, a search for "Teyonah Parris hair" on YouTube returns pages of tutorial

"I didn't associate how I looked in my natural state with beauty."

videos in which women attempt to recreate her various styles. Parris has also been diligent about helping change the perception of black lives through her performances on screen. She has actively pursued parts that were particularly important to her. She got the role in *Dear White People*, which tells the stories of black students at a predominantly white Ivy league college, because she asked for it: She knew writer/director Justin Simien and producer Lena Waithe and asked to be a part of the movie. "I knew Justin and Lena when we were all struggling and hustling out in LA, so when [*Dear White People*] started to happen, I said to Justin, 'Hey, I want to come in and audition.'" She's remained very pointed about the roles that she chooses, explaining, "It needs to be something that people can glean something from—that reflects something going on in their lives or in the world around them. Or that reveals someone else's truth so that people may have a better understanding of someone they may not meet."

Though she's specifically sought out collaborations with black directors, she was the one being chased to play one of her most influential roles: as Dawn, the first black recurring character on the hit series *Mad Men*, which centers on the lives of a mostly white advertising agency in 1960s New York. When asked about this specific character, Parris laughs and says it was pure luck that brought the role to her. At the time, she was a struggling actress in LA, sleeping on her teenage cousin's twin-size bunk bed, with only $1,200 to her name. She was considering a move back to New York when a friend invited her on a trip to India. She couldn't really afford it but booked a nonrefundable ticket anyway. Shortly after, she got the call to audition for Dawn—a character described as a "co-star, possibly recurring." She was supposed to be in India during the exact dates she would have to film, but

Above: Parris wears a double-breasted blazer by Derek Lam 10 Crosby and trousers by Irwin Garden.

she decided to audition anyway. Of course, Parris got the role. Dawn was introduced in the third episode of season five, when she submits her resumé to become a secretary for the show's lead character, Don Draper. It just so happened—for the first time in the show's history—that the series was filmed out of sequence, which meant that Parris could film the third episode and then go to India while they completed episodes one and two. When she came back from her trip, she was asked to return as Dawn. Looking back, she says, "That was nothing but God and his grace and his favor and luck." This is typical of Parris' attitude toward her success: "It's been hard work and discipline and dedication, facilitated and orchestrated by God the creator," she says. "My faith is the foundation on which all things that are Teyonah come from. My belief in God and his greater plan, my relationship with him is the foundation of my life. Period."

The *Mad Men* schedule clash also taught her the necessity of balancing her personal life with an increasingly busy professional career. "The nature of being an actor, performer or entertainer is that we're always looking for work. We're always trying to figure out what's next. Everything is a variable: 'Well if this goes well, then I might be in this city.' Everything is up in the air and you find yourself never feeling settled, never going to your niece's birthday because you might miss an audition, never going to sit with your family because maybe they'll call you back. You never really get to live. We need to take time for ourselves, to nurture relationships with family, friends and loved ones. That reflects in your work." Parris' most recent role is as Ernestine Rivers

FEATURES

"Hollywood can't be one group of people being able to tell their stories all the time."

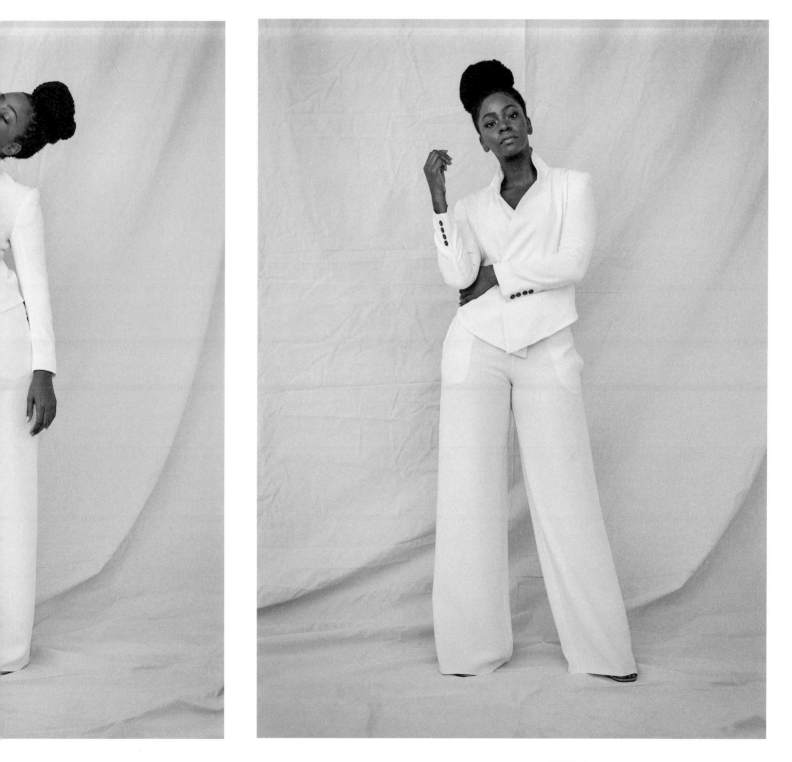

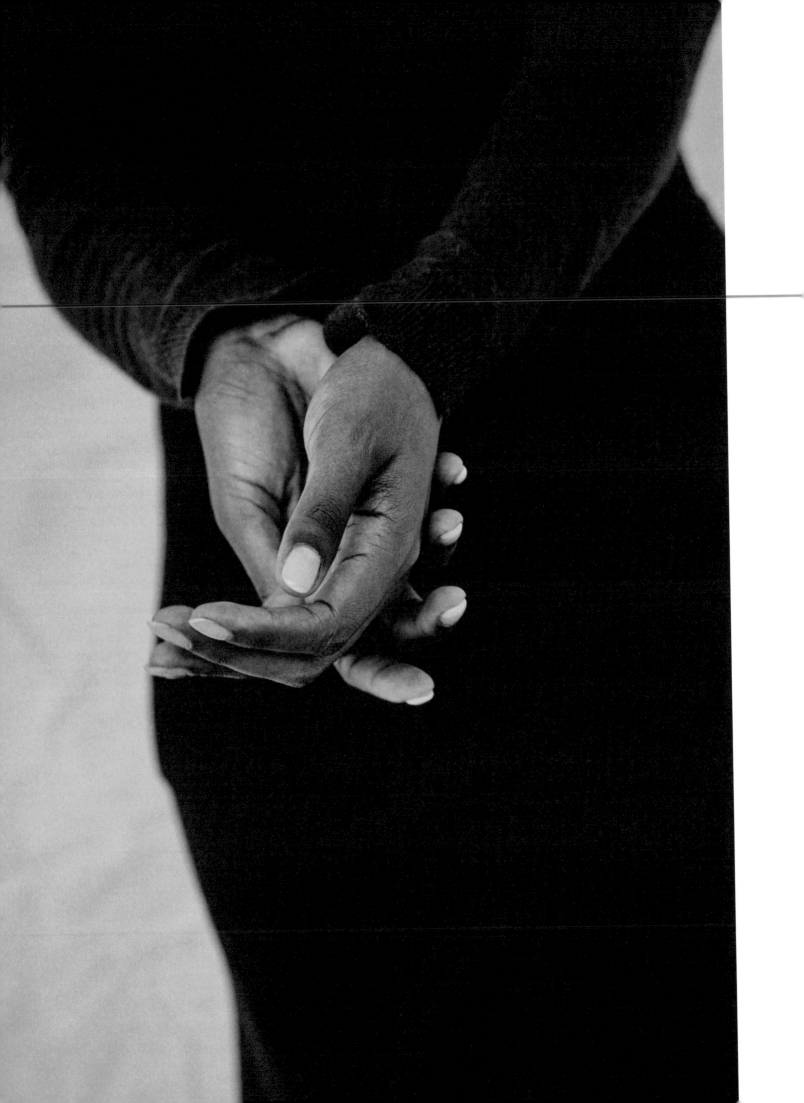

in Barry Jenkins' film adaptation of the James Baldwin classic *If Beale Street Could Talk*—a project that fills her with pride. "I'm a huge fan of James Baldwin. Just being able to get up there and say his words and bring his story to life was a blessing," she says. The film follows the story of Ernestine's pregnant sister Tish (Kiki Layne) and her fiancé Alonzo (Stephan James) as Alonzo is wrongfully accused and jailed for rape in the 1970s. Tish and Ernestine, along with their mother Sharon (Regina King), are forced to utilize their respective strengths to prove his innocence during what was a particularly racist period in United States history—one marked by police brutality, housing discrimination and mass incarceration.

The film bears even greater significance for Parris when she reflects on its parallels with the current political climate. "It's crazy because [Baldwin] wrote this over 40 years ago and—looking at what we're dealing with now—you would not know any difference, which is heartbreaking," she says. "I think it's important for black people to be seen in many different capacities and walks of life. That goes back to what I was saying about choosing things I want to be a part of. What does this say to the masses about who we are as a people and our different facets and ways in which you can be black and female in the world? I think this film deals with all of that."

When it comes to responding to situations of social and racial injustice (and if you follow her on social media, you know that she will *always* respond) Parris' passion is evident, albeit inflected with a politeness that reflects her South Carolina roots. In a 2016 interview with *The Huffington Post*, after the murders of Alton Sterling and Philando Castile at the hands of police officers, Parris implored white Americans to stand with black Americans in the fight against injustice: "Dear white people, when your black brothers and sisters are in pain and hurting, it also affects you. It would behoove you to help, be a voice, and stand in solidarity with them [against] these awful injustices, that are so clear to everyone via cell phone videos, and know that it matters."

Today, when asked whether she feels there's been any progress galvanizing white allies in the struggle for equality in Hollywood in the wake of the #TimesUp movement, when issues like the gender pay gap are at the forefront of many women's minds, she offers another characteristically considered response: "I think that it is important in the struggle—the struggle being pay equality, racial equality, gender equality—that white people position themselves as allies. What does that look like? That means amplifying the voice of those in need, learning about whatever their struggles are and asking how they can be of assistance."

There has been some improvement, she feels. "I do find it happening more. Specifically, when you see roles that were originally for actors of color or based on a book in which that character was Asian or black or whatever and somehow it got cast white. Those actors are now saying, 'Perhaps I shouldn't take this. Let me step out of the way so that I can be an ally to my fellow artists who may be more appropriate for the role as it was written or who don't typically have as much opportunity as someone like me'—typically a white man or a white female."

It's something Parris hopes will only get better. Already in 2018, there have been unprecedented options to see people of color on the big screen—which excited Parris. "I will be there for *Crazy Rich Asians*," she said at the time. "I will, and I should, and I hope that others will support them and their stories, and make sure that Hollywood and entertainment is not a monolith. It can't be one single story being told, or one group of people being able to tell their stories all the time. I'll also be there for *BlacKkKlansman*. I think it's important for us all to find a way to become an ally to those who need it."

She holds herself personally accountable: "I think that it's important for not only white allies, but for all people of color to be allies. Like my Asian and Hispanic brothers and sisters and artists, they all need more space and representation," she says. "They have even less than we as black people typically are given, less space to be seen and less stories that are told. So, I find myself making sure I'm an ally to them."

At 31 years old, Parris has become the role model she set out to be when watching Berry's iconic Oscar moment. Now she is hoping to find a new way to leave her mark—producing. "I want to be a part of getting those stories out," she says. "I want to find like-minded artists who have stories to tell and need a place to amplify their vision."

Left: Parris wears a turtleneck and dress by Agnona.

ACQUIRED TASTE

TEXT:
ELLIE VIOLET BRAMLEY

Taste has never existed in a vacuum. The things you like are influenced by the community around you, the people you admire from afar and the media you consume—this magazine, for example. But increasingly, it's also affected by non-sentient influencers—through computer calculations that prod us toward the things we "may also like." Ellie Violet Bramley asks: In the age of algorithms, can our taste ever be truly our own?

"Who runs the world?" Since 2011, millions of Beyoncé fans the world over have been ready with the answer: "Girls." The song has over 400 million views on YouTube and the album on which it appears has had more than a billion streams on Spotify.

This tells you something about who, or what, *really* runs the world: algorithms. It's at least in part down to these bite-size chunks of mathematics that culture now spreads so quickly and widely. They're the reason so many of us around the world have been exposed to the same material—in this case, the gospel according to Queen Bey.

In his influential essay *Style Is an Algorithm*, Kyle Chayka loosely defines algorithms as "sets of equations that work through machine learning to customize the delivery of content to individuals, prioritizing what they think we want, and evolving over time based on what we engage with." Elsewhere, they have been called the "secret sauce of a computerized world." They're shaping our lives without many of us realizing it.

Algorithms of different shapes and sizes map out our online journeys. Google's all-powerful algorithm PageRank decides which results appear at the top when you search—a potent role given how few of us flick beyond the first few pages of search results. Visit Netflix, as 125 million of us do worldwide, and you will be sorted into several taste groups among more than 2,000 before algorithms decide what to recommend based on these classifications—80 percent of the TV shows people watch on Netflix are "discovered" this way. On Amazon, algorithms will direct you to books it thinks you

will like: Just bought a Joan Didion, why not try a Maggie Nelson? Spotify's Discover Weekly playlist algorithm recommends tracks based in part on what you've already listened to, as well as on the artists you follow. On Instagram, with its 800 million users worldwide, algorithms figure out what you like and show you more of it—and the more likes a post has, the higher it'll appear on people's timelines. It's unsurprising that a photograph announcing that Beyoncé was expecting twins was 2017's most liked on the platform; her posts can rack up millions of likes within hours.

These lines of code impact what we watch, listen to, read and wear, as well as who we connect with. They're shaping the way we consume culture, and the way, in turn, culture is produced for our consumption; they are shaping our tastes. But what is taste, that it can seemingly be reduced to algorithms? From the band posters we had on our walls as teenagers to the books we have on our bedside tables now, the things we like create our sense of self. Yet we struggle to understand our attraction to them. In his 1979 book, *Taste*, Italian philosopher Giorgio Agamben writes that taste "enjoys beauty without being able to rationally account for it." One of the best modern books on taste, Tom Vanderbilt's *You May Also Like: Taste in an Age of Endless Choice*, echoes this idea: "We are strangers to our tastes," Vanderbilt writes.

Over email from New York, the author explains that, in his view, taste is "a sort of story we tell ourselves about our relationships with objects in the world and, importantly, our relationships with others and *their* relationships with objects—because without society, the no-

tion of taste rather falls apart." Taste, Vanderbilt says, is "entirely subjective, endlessly fleeting, open to all sorts of 'epigenetic' influences." Broadly, he says, "taste works according to a kind of associative sorting—you generally share the taste of people you find yourself amongst." In the past that might have meant your colleagues or neighbors, or—at a slight remove—your favorite radio DJ and the editor of a fashion magazine you read religiously. It could still mean all of those things, but it could also mean the different types of algorithms that serve you.

Are recommendation algorithms so different from a friend? Vanderbilt points out that taste has, historically, been dictated by algorithmic processes. "We read the books that others were reading, or that were in a genre we liked... or we flagged the fact that people in our school or workplace were suddenly wearing a certain brand of clothing," he argues. "Choices were typically based on past choices."

Theoretically, the internet should have expanded our choice networks: We now have access to endless amounts of music, films, fashion, art and writing from all over the world. The boundaries that kept culture, and its consumers, in their boxes have been blown off. "Taste is still divided along class lines but I think there's a degree of omnivorousness; we're all picking from a wider range now," says Simon Stewart, author of *A Sociology of Culture, Taste and Value*. "Upper class people are watching reality TV like everyone else—the taste barriers, you might say, have been blurred."

This is big news if you look at the history of taste. Long associated with class, it has, according to Vanderbilt, "often been felt more keenly as a *negative* force—strongly reacting to something one thinks is in 'poor taste.'" Taste has, throughout its history, been weaponized, made into a form of power and a means of exclusion—you might be dismissed for wearing the "wrong kind" of shoe or looked down on for liking techno rather than *La Traviata*.

So, has the internet created a cultural utopia where all can create, disseminate and consume freely and equally? Not quite. Instead, we are seeing what Chayka identifies as the replacement of the old dominant regime of mass-media television by a new taste regime powered by "Instagram likes, Twitter hashtags, and Google-distributed display advertising."

In a cultural landscape where we are inundated with options, recommendation algorithms that work on the principle of "if you like x, then you'll like y" can feel like trusty friends. They appear to know us. "I think people are endlessly tickled by that," says Ben Ratliff, author of *Every Song Ever: Twenty Ways to Listen in an Age of Musical Plenty*. "It's flattering." They guide us to things that sound, look or read a lot like material we're already familiar with. For Vanderbilt, "In an age of often bewildering choice in which I no longer have time to read back issues of *Cahiers du Cinéma* or flip through bins at the record store, there might be some benefit to off-loading some of my decision-making and discovery to a computer."

As Damon Krukowski, musician and author of *The New Analog: Listening and Reconnecting in a Digital World*, describes it, these companies "use the illusion of choice, because the idea of choice is seductive, but the fact of choice is

actually not so popular... It takes a lot of individual work."

The problem with outsourcing our choices is that it can narrow them according to what we have already consumed. As Chayka puts it, the promise of algorithms is: "If you like this, you will get more of it, forever." This logic is shown to be absurd when targeted ads insist on recommending to us the items (a toilet seat, a new lamp, a mother's day gift) that we've just bought. The narrowing effect of algorithmic predictions has led to what Ratliff calls "bottomless comfort zones." Speaking over the phone from his home in the Bronx he expands: "The business of the streaming services is to take care of your taste. They're going to keep you engaged, amused, up-to-date... basically you'll just be entertained forever." Sound good? Don't be fooled, says Ratliff. The rub is that you'll be a customer for life at the expense of real cultural discovery, thanks to the lines the algorithms have drawn in the digital sand: "It's sort of an illusion of surprise because real surprise would be 'Oh, you like Drake, well there's this composer from the 12th century named Hildegard von Bingen....'"

The impact of algorithms on culture and taste itself have been multifaceted. In some quarters there's been a blandification. Writing in *The Baffler*, Liz Pelly charts the rise of "chill" music on Spotify's algorithmically designed playlists, a genre she calls the "purest distillation of its ambition to turn all music into emotional wallpaper." As we become passengers on our own cultural journeys we partake in what digital strategists call "lean back listening"; we have become sufficiently anesthe-

tized as to want more and more beige playlists.

While the internet in some senses throws culture wide open by giving unprecedented access and encouraging the omnivorousness that Stewart looks to, it can also have a flattening effect. Culture has effectively been globalized, says Dr. Safiya Umoja Noble, an assistant professor at the University of Southern California whose work examines the intersection between technology and cultural bias. Noble points out that there have, of course, been earlier hegemonic cultural drivers: the export of British culture throughout its former empire, for example. "[But] the scale and speed are significantly different now," she says; the internet knows no bounds. Speaking over the phone from Accra, she can attest that Bey-mania is alive in Ghana: "I can't tell you how much Chris Brown, Beyoncé and Justin Bieber I'm hearing here," she says. "American capital, in particular in the entertainment industry, is powerful and global in its reach." And Google, she says, "is going to amplify that rather than suppress it because it is a major player in that amplification."

Elsewhere, algorithms are giving birth to strange new cultural hybrids. In the world of fashion, Stitch Fix is using algorithms not simply to pick clothes for users but also to help design them, creating garments based on the most popular characteristics of users' clothes. It's been called "algo-clash clothing": If people report a love of two distinct details—peplums and florals, say—why not combine the two? It's Frankenstein's monster in fashion.

They might even be used to inform the kinds of books that are being published. If, as several data-driven start-ups have claimed,

"As we become passengers on our own cultural journeys we partake in what digital strategists call 'lean back listening'; we have become sufficiently anesthetized as to want more and more beige playlists."

machine classification algorithms can be used to isolate the features most common in bestsellers—"human closeness," a young, strong heroine and dogs—then why not commission more of the same and double down on what's been popular in the past?

But if all this makes you worry that algorithms are on an unstoppable march to homogenize our lives, take comfort. Algorithms are never perfect—especially when it comes to the fiddly question of personal taste—and this limitation may well prove their undoing. Take the algorithm that dishes up the Spotify Discover Weekly playlist. Yes, plenty of people celebrate its magic, its ability to know the listener well. But it doesn't *always* hit the taste nail on the head. And at that moment when the nail goes in wonky, the spell can be broken. Often, when Ratliff looks at his playlist, he feels revulsion. He explains, "Something has determined what I like, my sort of musical personality quite closely, but of course it's not me. And it's disgusting actually, it makes me want to run away from whatever music they're pushing on me." He likens the effect to the phenomenon of the uncanny valley, a sensation defined as "a common unsettling feeling people experience when androids and audio/visual simulations closely resemble humans but are not quite convincingly realistic." There's a reason they miss the mark: "They're not really geared to *you* per se," Ratliff says. "They're geared to your approximate data set."

As we become more aware of the workings of algorithms, we are also becoming savvier to the fact that they serve many masters. "The economic imperative still prevails," says Stewart.

"Algorithms can be used to navigate and explore but I don't think it's always in the interests of these companies to tell you exactly what you like because they've also been paid to advertise particular artists such as Drake."

Profit lies in the narrowing of choices, hence the emphasis Spotify places on playlists rather than the wide-open terrain of its back catalog. According to Krukowski, "They're working hard to encourage us to use it … in the way that's more profitable for them, more controllable and lower cost, too." He relates it to Netflix, which steers us toward its own original series. "The profit is to be had in the product that they control and they own," he says. So, it seems we'll all watch more *House of Cards* and less of *The West Wing*.

Another deep flaw is that algorithms have the effect of being anti-progress. As Joy Buolamwini, a researcher at the MIT Media Lab and founder of the Algorithmic Justice League, puts it: "Our past dwells in [algorithms]". It's a phenomenon she refers to as the "coded gaze," where biases—racial, sexual—are baked into the machines. And it's obvious why—as Noble, author of *Algorithms of Oppression*, explains: "Ask a computer scientist, what is an algorithm, they'll say a certain kind of applied mathematical formulation or a sorting mechanism… [but] an algorithm cannot think, so people have to nuance it. And, of course, one of the things we know is that many people who write algorithms are in this very narrow band of mostly white and Asian men."

What might this mean for our cultural landscape? The idea that Spotify upholds the music industry status quo is nothing new. Writing

again in *The Baffler*, Pelly looks to whether "gender bias would be reproduced through algorithmic recommendations like Discover Weekly" and finds that in total, on these algorithmic playlists artists were 79.2 percent male and 12.5 percent female. And consider that Netflix has been shown to only offer users "black" content once they have expressed a specific interest in it. It's no wonder that Noble believes in the importance of training the people designing the algorithms to have a better understanding of their impact: "Why wouldn't we ask computer scientists to have a degree in ethnic studies or women's studies?"

As individual consumers of culture, we can rebel against the algorithm by remaining alert to culture and to our own tastes rather than allowing ourselves to become compliant passengers. Aim for what Chayka describes as "content Luddism"—the ethical sourcing of culture. That might take the form of only reading the dustiest books at your local thrift shop rather than meekly accepting Amazon's recommendations. As we become more aware of the heavy hands of algorithms on what should be a very human faculty—taste—we will become better equipped for the job of raging against the machine.

Ratliff is certainly trying. "Lately I do think a lot about what someone of my dataset generally doesn't listen to. I play little games with myself. I look at that Spotify Discover Weekly playlist and I think about who that dude is that they're furnishing this for and I think I'd like to listen to music that that guy doesn't listen to."

So what would someone with your dataset *not* normally read, wear, watch? Try seeking those things out; you might surprise yourself.

Day in the Life:
Amah Ayivi

In Paris, *Sarah Moroz* meets an entrepreneurial flaneur who has pivoted from casting director, to restaurateur, to vintage clothing importer—all while staying true to his own singular style. Photography by *Lasse Fløde*

"I'm wearing cook's pants," Amah Ayivi says, pointing at his slender checkered trousers. Earlier in the morning, they caused some confusion at the bakery where he buys his morning croissant. He laughs at the memory. Whether in partial chef uniform or not, Ayivi attracts attention. Even now, while seated in a Parisian café just down the street from his showroom, three people and a dog greet him warmly within an hour.

Today, paired with his trousers are a slim white T-shirt, a gray-and-white hat and plastic jellies. He has a vast assortment of silver rings on all fingers, including one that declares ART COMES FIRST (from the eponymous brand), several from Morocco and Niger plus a woman's ring by American jeweler Ginette that lives on his pinky. His style reveals his sense of limitlessness. "People have this *idée arrêtée*"—fixed idea," he says. "For me, you can wear whatever you want. If you're good with it, then it's okay." While acknowledging that it's the image of the chic Parisian that people around the world are most familiar with, Ayivi insists that true French style is "bohème." He, of course, falls squarely in that camp: In the streets, as on Instagram, strangers praise him daily. "Style is also a way to talk to people," he says.

A charismatic dandy and inveterate bargain-hunter, Ayivi was born in Togo and arrived in France in 1983 at the age of 11, accompanied by his uncle, while his parents remained in Africa. His style had been shaped by his father: by following him to the tailor, choosing fabrics at the market, and seeing him dazzle in the resulting three-piece suits. In Paris, Ayivi grew up in the city's northern quarter, not far from the famous Marché aux Puces de Saint-Ouen, which he would regularly comb for antique treasures.

Ayivi began his career in marketing, then realized he hated office life. A friend's cousin, who worked at a production company, needed someone who could rally an interesting crowd for a music video: "bring the *réseau*"—network—"to the set," as Ayivi puts it. That, he could do. He continued to cast professionally over a period of nine years, peopling the music videos of French hip-hop stars with interesting figures he encountered. He relied on instinct rather than modelling agencies: "In the street, you can find this kind of... attitude," he explains. But with the rise of social media, approaches to professional casting changed: "The producer just has to post an ad, and they get lots of people who want to do it for free."

Through his eclectic import business, Ayivi hopes to correct the French misperception that patterned wax fabrics are Africa's sole contribution to textiles.

"Wear whatever you want. Style is a way to talk to people."

"Wear whatever you want. Style is a way to talk to people."

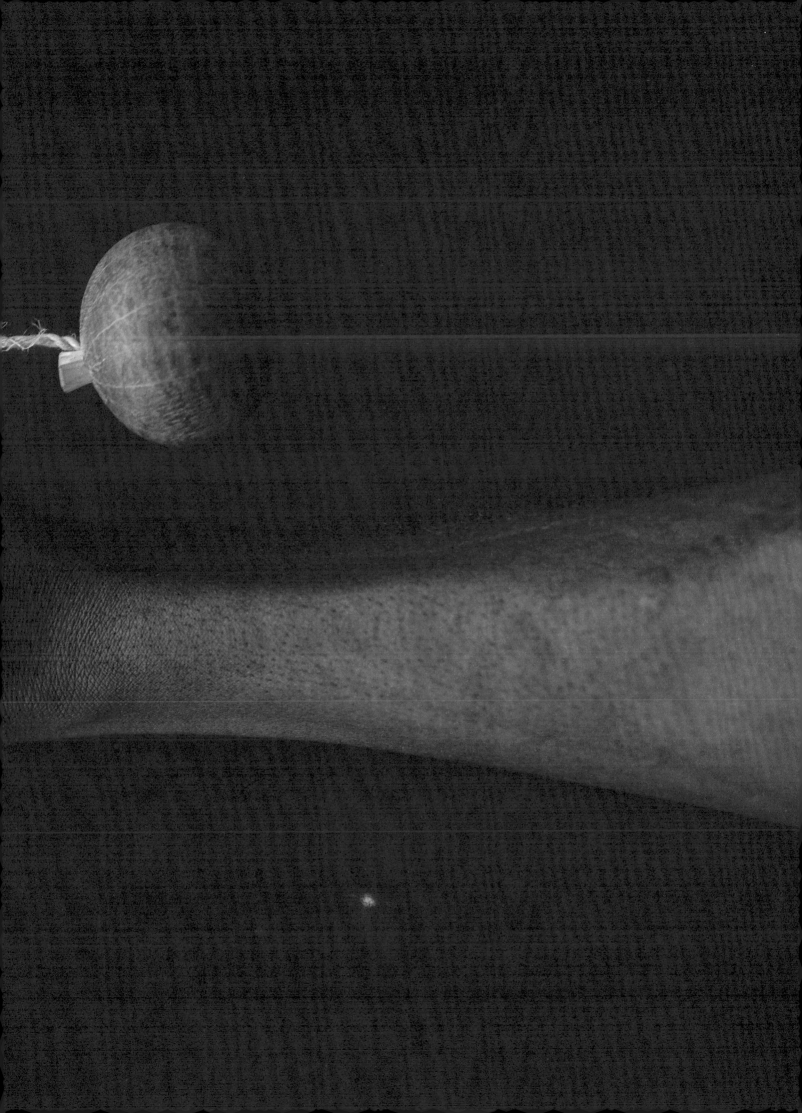

He pivoted. For two years, he ran his own African restaurant. Then he moved to Comptoir Général—a sprawling 6,500-square-foot venue off the Canal Saint-Martin inspired by the vibes of Francophone Africa and the Carribean. Ayivi thought it was not developing to its full potential as a community and commercial hub, so he brokered a meeting with the founder, Aurélien Laffon, and suggested the addition of an "Afrobrunch"—eggs with onions and tomato, mango juice, toasted pineapple—as a draw. Laffon implemented it, and it was a success. Ayivi became further involved in the workings of the venue, including doing recruitment ("like casting," he notes).

On the mezzanine level of the venue, Ayivi opened a second-hand boutique, starting with 1,000 euros' worth of stock he bought from a wholesaler friend in Marseille. The endeavor took off quickly, and he needed more merchandise. He decided to source from Africa—albeit in a roundabout way. Rather than importing what might be considered "traditional" fabrics, he bought clothes from the Western nonprofit associations, such as the Red Cross, who supply tons upon tons of donated European clothes to wholesalers in Africa. Ayivi spends one month a year scouting markets in his native Togo for these donated wares. He buys items from the mid-'80s and earlier, and brings up to three tons of vintage clothing with him back to Europe. It's a peculiar circulatory system of export and import that reflects the fluctuations of the global market and regional tastes. "We like mostly new clothing—modern—and hate used vintage," Ayivi says of African sartorial tendencies. "When they see me, they say, 'You're going to wear that? You're crazy,'" he chuckles.

Ayivi's success at Le Comptoir Général led to a stand-alone boutique concept that migrated to the Marais district. Marché Noir opened in February 2016, selling second-hand clothing, plus coffee and juices in an adjoining café. But the venue wasn't licensed to stay open at night or sell alcohol, and so the café flailed and eventually closed down. "When you'd come to the shop, you'd go to the café. When you'd come to the café, you'd go to the shop. After we closed the café, it changed the business," Ayivi recalls. The whole endeavor folded in August 2017, and he split from Le Comptoir Général.

Since January, Ayivi has been holding court on rue des Gravilliers, a peculiar part of the Marais where mostly anonymous wholesalers are starting to be joined by trendier spots (a vegan pizza joint, a café selling 10-euro matcha drinks). At the showroom, his vintage pieces are on display alongside a line of brightly striped tote bags and workman jackets. He has also spearheaded a capsule collection of cotton tunics inspired by those traditionally worn in Ghana. Upstairs, he shares an office with a creative communications agency.

Ayivi hopes to open a new concept store—a *lieu de vie*, with food and drink—near the Place de la Bastille. He wants it to be a "laboratory": to host gatherings, to have a photo studio in which to shoot collections and welcome neighborhood associations. Inspired by Malick Sidibé—the Malian photographer who used to instruct the youth of Bamako to "Prenez la pose"—he'd like his studio to be a space where anyone can play. Such a venue is "about an experience and lifestyle," he says. "I don't want people to just come, buy and leave."

Designers, including Jean Paul Gaultier and Yves Saint Laurent, have long taken ideas from Africa, but often in a short-lived, trend-driven manner: "One season, then nothing," notes Ayivi. "Now, you have more African designers and artists showing differently. The energy is unbelievable," he says, referencing fashion shows in Lagos and emerging labels like LaurenceAirline. "The potential is huge. I want to keep my business growing there."

The West, he says, still clings to Africa as a struggling place. Indeed, the French department store Galeries Lafayette did a spotlight on contemporary African creativity, for which Ayivi consulted on art direction. But although the show featured young African artists, Galeries Lafayette called on European retailers to design an African-inspired collection, instead of tapping actual African designers to make merchandise. "You cannot say, 'We are doing African month,' without putting African designers in there," Ayivi points out.

What does he make of the fact that the crowd at Le Comptoir Général, while enchanted by its African themes, is unlikely to go to the actual African neighborhoods in Paris? The venue arguably accommodates a certain Western fantasy. It doesn't faze Ayivi: "People said it was like in the colonial days, because black people worked there and white people were the consumers." He shakes his head. "People go too far."

But Ayivi does want to confound the perception of Africa, swapping out thoughtless exoticism for regional celebration. His next project is an independently made, self-produced show highlighting contemporary African vision. Using two cameras, he intends to film across 15 to 20 African countries, making short videos about untapped milieus like the surf scene in Senegal, the electro music scene in Mali, luxury lifestyle in Lagos. "Africa is not just about traditional dance and music," he said. Nor is it a fleeting source of "cool." Ayivi himself can attest to this firsthand.

Fitting

In fashion, the first runway is the designer's atelier. Photography by Pelle Crepin & Styling by David Nolan

Above: Malik wears a shirt, jacket and tie by Brooks Brothers, trousers by Anderson & Sheppard and eyewear by General Eyewear. Left: Bibi wears a dress by Shushu/Tong, shoes by Marques'Almeida and earrings by COS. Previous spread: Bibi wears a dress by DAKS.

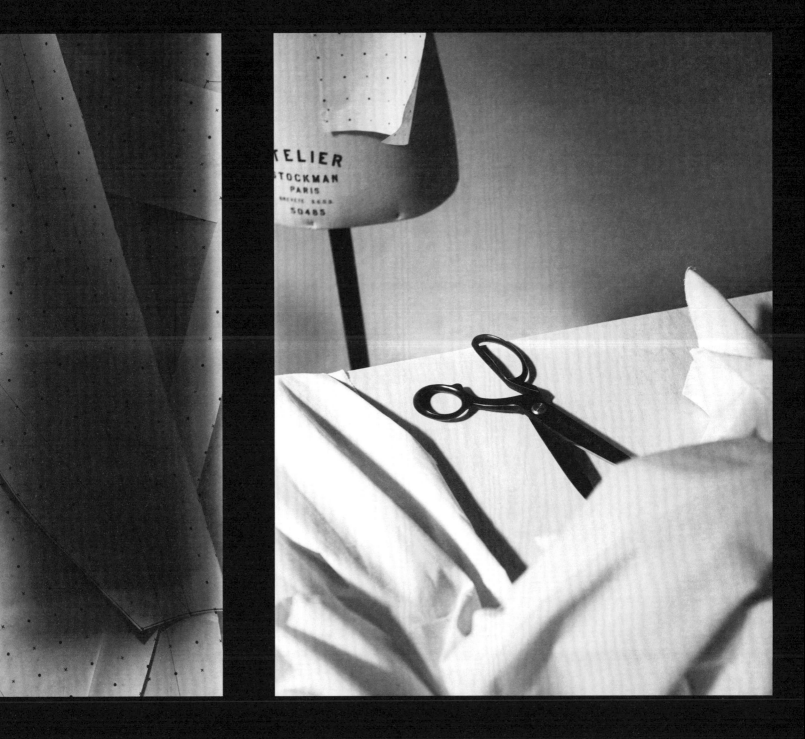

Above: Waxed threads and fabric shears from Labour And Wait.

Below: Malik wears a jacket by Maison Margiela and uses tailor's chalk from Labour And Wait. Right: He wears a shirt by Corneliani, a suit by Sandro, a tie by Brooks Brothers and a belt and pocket square by Anderson & Sheppard.

Above: Bibi wears a dress and underskirt by Ryan Lo. Right: Malik wears a knit by Neil Barrett, a suit by Paul Smith and eyewear by General Eyewear.
Bibi wears a dress and underskirt by Ryan Lo, a brassiere by Agent Provocateur and earrings by COS.

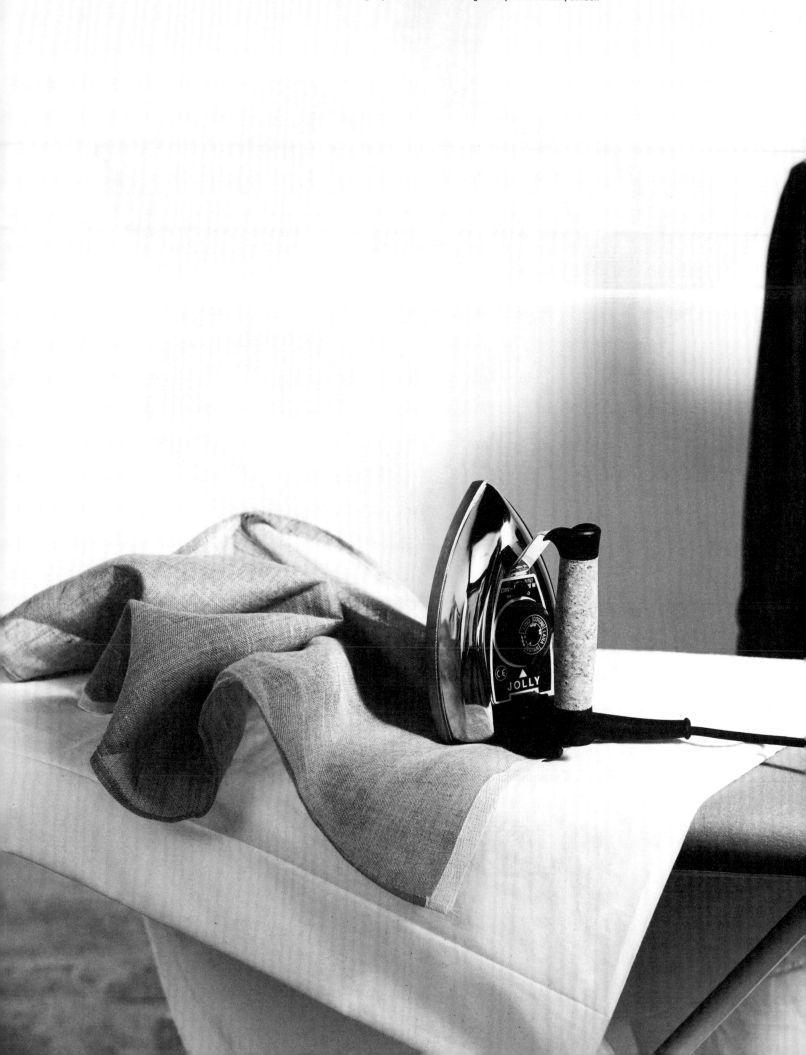

Left: Bibi wears a dress and skirt by Shushu/Tong and earrings by COS. Overleaf: She wears a dress by Loewe, boots by JW Anderson and earrings by COS. Below: Tailoring Iron by Norris Steam, London

M[ ]

MAISON
DE
VERRE

A cubist tableau. A light show. A maverick of modernism. *Hugo Macdonald* explores a Parisian masterpiece.

Photography by *François Halard* & *Dominique Vellay*

Hidden in an enclosed courtyard on rue Saint-Guillaume, in Paris' seventh arrondissement, is a house of holy grail status for the architecture community. In description alone, it sounds like something from a fairy tale: a glowing, three-story home made from glass bricks, wedged under the fourth-floor apartment of an 18th-century townhouse. The fact that it lay dormant for decades, unseen by all but a handful of family members and their friends, only adds to its legend.

The Maison de Verre is designed in the modernist tradition, but its hard lines and industrial materials are tempered by curves and soft textures.

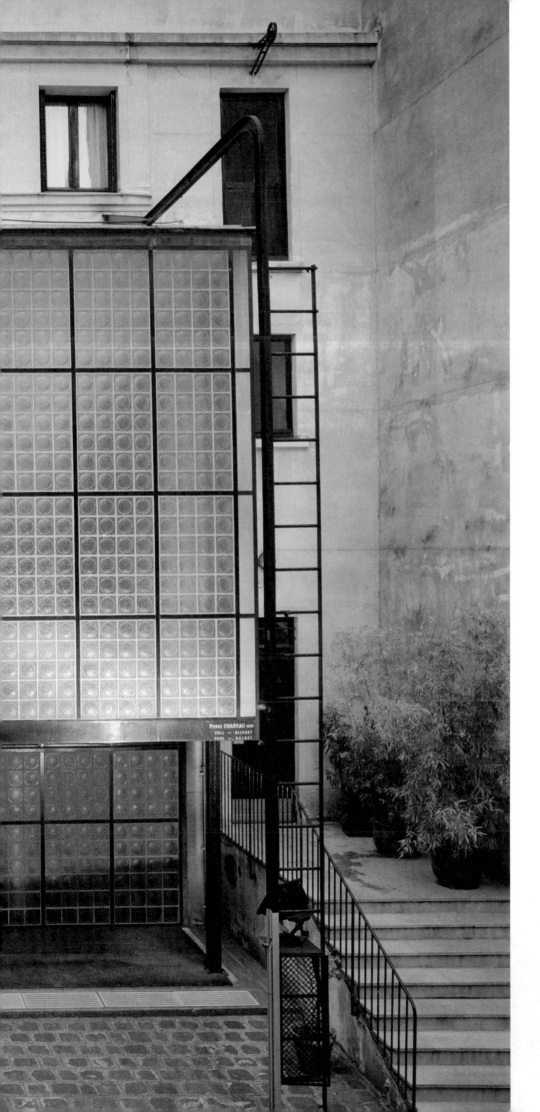

Even today, to visit the Maison de Verre you need to apply months in advance with proof of a connection to the profession of architecture. To call this house precious is an understatement. It is the sole surviving building (of only four completed) by the French architect Pierre Chareau. Built between 1927 and 1932 for Jean and Annie Dalsace, the house is an outstanding example of creative patronage. It is testament to Chareau's imagination and skill, but perhaps more to the friendship between the architect and client: An extraordinary level of trust would have been required to commission this experimental home.

The Dalsaces were an enlightened couple. Jean was a gynecologist who would in later life be an active promoter of contraception and found the French National Association for the Study of Abortion. Annie mixed in the avant-garde cultural circles of the time: "She was less interested in pearl necklaces and fur coats than in the works of Braque, Ernst and Picasso," her granddaughter Dominique Vellay wrote in a publication about the house.

It was thanks to Annie, more than Jean, that the Maison de Verre came into existence. Annie had met Louise Dyte, Pierre Chareau's English wife, in 1905. As well as teaching Annie to speak English, Louise introduced her to the progressive Parisian artists, musicians and writers that she and her husband mixed with and the two couples became close friends. It was Annie's parents who funded the work at Rue Saint-Guillaume in 1927, and Annie who was the open mind and driving force behind Chareau's creation.

The Maison de Verre has a peculiar infill setting, thanks to a tenant on the top floor of the existing building who refused to budge. Undeterred, Chareau propped up the apartment, demolished the rest of the building underneath it and constructed a double-height, open plan space out of steel girders in its place.

Architect Pierre Chareau imagined the house as a "cabinet" because of its glass facade.

He wrapped the courtyard-facing facade in translucent glass bricks, from which the house takes its name. It is said that he wanted the house to be "a box of light."

It is hard to emphasize the imagination, not to mention the bravery, behind these moves. Despite the mind expansion of cultural innovation sweeping through western Europe in the 1920s, the principles of modernist architecture were stark. Buildings tended to adhere to strict theories of process and function; they did not play freely with form and feeling. "The Maison de Verre is a whimsical place, a tour de force and a site of contradictions," says Esther da Costa Meyer, Professor of Architecture at Princeton University, who curated an exhibition on the house at the Jewish Museum in New York. "Today we are used to houses with glass facades but at the time, they were new."

She also underscores the inventiveness of the building on the inside: "Though Chareau produced elegant bespoke furniture for the house, the interior was full of mass-produced industrial materials exposed to view: rubber flooring, metal doors, exposed pipes, industrial lighting fixtures." If the exterior of the house was unusual for the time, the interior was another world entirely.

The girder supporting structure of the building meant that large spaces could be left open, concrete floors appeared to float and different spaces could be opened up or sectioned off with moving screens, all bathed in translucent light from the glass bricks on one side, with occasional flashes of views out to the garden on the opposite side. The effect is a house that feels like it is alive and changing constantly, with the movement of walls and parts, of light, and of people through it. It is the closest we might get to experiencing life inside a cubist painting.

Some have questioned if the need for sectioning off private from professional space was Chareau's starting point for including so many moving parts within the building: One of the construction requirements was a consultation and surgery space for Dr. Dalsace's private medical practice on the ground floor. But more likely it was thanks to Chareau's clients' proclivity for playfulness and the opportunity they presented to experiment widely with his collaborators, the genius metalworker Louis Dalbet and Dutch architect Bernard Bijvoet. "Dalbet handcrafted all the metal parts: the ventilation louvers in the living room, the retractable stairs in Madame Dalsace's bedroom, the incredible elements in the bathrooms," da Costa Meyer explains. Movable aluminum panels like airplane wings separate Jean's shower space from Annie's bath space.

There is an infectious sense of fun that runs throughout the Maison de Verre. This is a house with charm and charisma in every detail, from the phone booth with a light operated underfoot, to the aluminum coat hangers shaped like moustaches and the single red button by the entrance that lights the house on a timer, allowing just enough time to make it from the front door to the bedrooms. There are moments of ethereal beauty, surprising joy and utter genius intertwined. Yet, for all of its unusual character and ingenuity, the house has considerable domestic intimacy and comfort, too. Chareau balanced his use of industrial materials with natural ones: Pirelli rubber flooring and metal grate stairs are softened elsewhere with wood, slate and polished lacquer. Surfaces are smooth to touch and hard edges have been rounded. There's a surprising blue carpet in the less surprisingly named blue sitting room. Tapestry screens and embroidered upholstery by Jean Dalsace's school friend Jean Lurçat bring tactile layers of intrigue. What can look cold in photographs feels warm in the flesh.

Chareau also designed all the furniture and lighting in the house (except an early 19th-century mahogany dining table and set of chairs). This means the interior works perfectly with the architecture and, given his intimate friendship with the Dalsaces, he was able to create a world that they could inhabit effortlessly, however radical it might have been at the time. "The house was a place of friendship and open to everyone," Dominique Vellay remembers. The Alsaces' granddaughter later moved into the Maison de Verre with her daughter. "It was a meeting place where avant-garde ideas, artistic concepts and the most beautiful of utopian ideals could be expressed." She remembers her grandmother as the lady of the house, standing at the top of the stairs waiting to receive guests. She recalls the dinners, the parties, the music concerts. Interesting people were always passing through.

When the Germans occupied Paris in the Second World War, the Dalsaces and the Chareaus fled to America. The Maison de Verre was stripped of its furniture, which was hidden in a barn by a relative in rural France. The story goes that the Germans tried to requisition the house, but gave up when they realized they could neither heat it nor light it. After the war, the Dalsaces returned and the home stayed in the family until 2006, when it was sold to Robert Rubin, an American collector and investor-turned-architect. Rubin has meticulously restored it and lives there with his French wife and their children. Pierre Chareau stayed in America and built just two further projects in his life, neither of which remain today. It is a testament to the genius of the Maison de Verre that it has, by itself, cemented its creator's legacy as a maverick in the canon of modern architecture.

Chareau was driven to create entire environments rather than individual items. In the 1920s, he worked as a set designer on films including *Le Vertige* and *L'Argent*.

REVOLUTIONARY DESIGN

by Harriet Fitch Little

"People in glass houses shouldn't throw stones." It's a saying that Jean Dalsace must surely have had in mind when he commissioned Chareau to build his Maison de Verre. A devoted member of the French Communist party, Dalsace wanted to design a space that reflected his desire for radical transparency: a salon where the most important ideas of the 1930s could be illuminated by its greatest minds. Artist-intellectuals including Cocteau, Picasso and Miró all held court. Walter Benjamin, who knew the house well, was inspired by its construction to consider the political import of architecture: "To live in a glass house is a revolutionary virtue par excellence," he wrote.

Serendipity marked Eileen Myles' discovery of the St. Mark's Poetry Project upon moving to New York City in 1974. Hosting readings by Allen Ginsberg and workshops taught by Alice Notley, the Poetry Project gave Myles a poetic education that complemented a long-held passion for literature, performance, music, and creative communities. The writing career that resulted resists fixed definitions and includes lauded poetry collections such as *Not Me*, the autobiographical novel *Chelsea Girls* and the genre-defying *Afterglow: A Dog Memoir*, which opens with an accusatory letter from a lawyer representing Myles' late pit bull, Rosie. "Maybe as an ex-Catholic, I kind of fear becoming something too much," they joke.

"They" is Myles' preferred pronoun because of the multiplicity it represents. "I feel female and male, and neither part is abandoned by 'they,'" Myles declares. "When someone calls me Miss or Ma'am, I feel pissed; if they say Sir, I think I'm going to get caught. Neither is right. Not for me."

Once a fringe poet, Myles has now found a mainstream audience and critical recognition; Yale University recently bought their archives.

Now asserting a general collective identity, Myles, in 1991, tried representing a particular collective by running for president of the United States. "There wasn't any possibility that there would be a female candidate, a gay candidate, an artist candidate, a candidate making under $50,000 a year, a minority candidate," they would later explain. Though Myles lost, they have continued resisting the status quo and asserting the presence and voices of those othered. In turn, they have continually reached new audiences, most recently through Cherry Jones' character in Amazon's *Transparent* who was inspired by Myles. Shifting seamlessly between trenchant political commentary, humor and poignant observation, they illuminate with delicate and often arresting precision not just life's messiness but also the fantastical nature of our most quotidian activities.

Much of your work and commentary concerns your frustration and anger regarding politics, the mistreatment of female and queer bodies, among other critical topics. But in *Evolution*, you write "the world is never superfluous" and dancing appears frequently—even your titles are "wiggling." Are you optimistic, at least about everyday existence? Sometimes you have to accept absolutely how bad things are to bring on a transition. Years ago, one really hot summer day, I was walking through my neighborhood doing errands in a sort of hell; suddenly, I had a thought, which I just had to mentally repeat: "It will always be this way. It will always be this way." What was so weird was that it created a kind of air conditioner, this total acceptance of how I felt utterly condemned.

Everything has limits. Whether it's politics or Buddhism, evil is kind of a state of mind, and if we don't agree to live there, it ceases to exist in a very real way.

Some people call social media a kind of hell. How do you feel about the digital world, with its proliferation of text? It's sure great for poets. Having a poem in *The New Yorker* is nice, but people really want to know that it's on the web, too, and available to everybody. The digital world works with the fragmentation of consciousness and aligns poetry with that. We're having a heyday in poetry that I think will last a very long while because it's the very consciousness which people are speaking in today. It wasn't that way 20 years ago. It's also great and kind of nuts that

"When a poet dies, everyone gets up and reads their work. We're like a big cover band."

so many people come to me and other poets now through Instagram—that pictures lead them to words.

Poems are about desire, you've said. Are reading and writing inherently erotic? On one hand, a poem is just a list of things, and a list is often about what I want. That can go off on many tangents, with lists about forgetfulness, ecstasy, shopping. It's an open-ended tool.

But think also about the history of language: People suggest the first language is poetry. It was a sort of magical utterance, one up from animal sounds but repeated, which creates an altered state. That's very similar to sex and sexuality. Talking scores sex. You don't talk constantly, but people say things at important points, and they have effects.

That emphasis on sound foregrounds the musicality of words, too. How does your writing relate to music? I don't play any musical instruments, yet there's a way in which my poetry is that longing to make sounds. The way I imagine sound is pretty fantastic. The real performance is the act of writing itself—you're weaving and bobbing through all these strata. There's nothing more exciting than the first time I get to read a piece aloud. It reiterates that moment when I was conceiving it and hopefully realizes it because when I'm reading I hope people listening can lift the work off the page forevermore. *That* corresponds to music, which always has the capacity to fill space.

But too often people don't want to listen, especially if what you're reading is considered "difficult." For a long time, the mainstream publishing world published the "official poets," and the weirdos and experimentalists were outside of that to a large extent. One can be changing language a little too fast for the institutions of literature, and that's a kind of badness. In the very act of making a poem, poets protect us. We're making small revolutionary acts, a nest where we can show dangerous things. We can hide things; we can create a code of information. For a while, political poetry was not the mode—there was a sense that, even if you were an avant-garde poet, you didn't want to be carrying a message. That conflict doesn't exist anymore. Messages can contradict and occupy the same space, which means you don't have to make a poem a guided missile. It's like comedy in its way.

A poet is—almost by definition—unable to work in isolation. How important is community to your work? Lots of poets probably love the idea that they learned to write poetry alone, but that's not my experience at all. I studied in workshops, read in open readings and published in anthologies. Even when I first went to artist colonies, I had a hard time sitting in my studio and writing all day. I was so used to writing a poem, getting on the phone with a friend and reading it. Developing work apart was very hard for me. I didn't have that support to go out on a long path by myself; I needed somebody to catch me.

When a poet dies, everyone gets up and reads their work; that's how we memorialize them. We're like a big cover band! There's nothing more pleasurable than covering your favorite poem in public, hearing it aloud. There isn't so much a fashion today of reading each other's work at poetry readings, but whenever anybody does it, it blows people away.

You built much of that community for yourself when you moved to New York. But do you agree with critics who label you a "New York poet"? I do to the extent that I became myself in New York, so New York in many ways turned me into *me*. The city's "too muchness" advocated a permanent sense of multiplicity of ways of making art; it always felt that instead of being stuck with this situation or that group, you could just move slightly. New York is my aesthetic, too, but in many ways, the city that made me isn't there anymore—and then it also is.

When I first went to Rome, it was weird how many time periods were present at once. New York has some of that, but it's so piggish. We just knock anything down, and it's shocking what isn't preserved and what is, accidentally.

I kind of embrace and deny the idea of being a "New York poet." The first time I went to write at the country home of some artist friends, what was so exciting was to bring my way of writing to nature and realize that nature isn't so different from the city. The city's way of piling incident on was happening in nature, but just in a softer way.

In some languages adjectives follow nouns, making you a "poet" above all else. Does that appeal to you more? I hate adjectives. They weigh down the flow and predetermine things way too much, wherever they are in a sentence. The little words you jam in lessen, giving people the option to say "I don't like that" in this in/out way. Women and queers often get a quick description of how to understand them. I want to be amplified in terms of possibility! I want to be a paragraph, not just a word! But if it's going to be a word, I want it to be something that will throw you a curve. Dennis Cooper called me "one of the... most restless intellects in contemporary literature." I really liked that, because the thing is not to sit there being bored—just *go*.

The 2015 rerelease of *Chelsea Girls* introduced Myles' writing to a new generation.

"So many people come to poets now through Instagram—pictures lead them to words."

At Work With:
Nadège Vanhée-Cybulski

Hermès' womenswear designer gets color inspiration from art, sketches on her iPad and treats designing clothes like filmmaking. At Paris' Hôtel de Crillon, she talks to *Sarah Moroz* about helming a heritage house. Photography by *Luc Braquet*

When Nadège Vanhée-Cybulski was named artistic director of Hermès' women's ready-to-wear in 2014, she disrupted an all-male lineage at the French luxury *maison* that ran through Christophe Lemaire, Jean Paul Gaultier and Martin Margiela. She also had kept a relatively low profile, having previously worked behind the scenes at Maison Martin Margiela and Céline, and then for three years as women's design director at The Row.

But the French-born designer, who trained at the Royal Academy of Fine Arts in Antwerp, doesn't seem easily flappable. Her gentle manner is paired with firm confidence, whether she's pairing trainers with swim-suits at work or enjoying bad movies as much as art house ones at home.

When did you know you wanted to work in fashion? I think design has always been considered a very noble job, but 25 years ago fashion was not as popular as it is today, so I came to it gradually. As a young wom-an I think you really educate yourself through your circle of friends. I see fashion as cultural and anthropological—I like to see the way dif-ferent civilizations have embedded their specificity through costumes or tailoring or embellishment. And I felt a great affinity with the Ant-werp school, because they were offering a really demanding program: crafting a collection, different *passerelles* [bridges] between disciplines… I felt drawn to this type of education.

Did you make your own clothes when you were younger? No, I was more of a stylist. My best friend and I would spend Saturdays at differ-ent vintage stores and flea markets, and then we would dress up. When I started to feel more comfortable with garment construction, I would alter my own clothes.

Recently, there was an exhibition exploring Margiela's work during his Hermès years. How would you present *your* Hermès years, if you could? I am too young to do a retrospective… but what I'm obsessed with in the Hermès wardrobe is definitely the silk. The silk shirt really comes from transforming a silk scarf, and I would love to do an exhibition about that. And the exceptional leather pieces are a red thread for me: super-thin leather trench coats, or beautiful dresses that are half-leather, half-tweed.

"I see fashion as anthropological. Civilizations have embedded their specificity through costume."

Vanhée-Cybulski explains Hermès' French heritage in terms of "terroir" — a term used by winemakers to describe the impact of environment on an end product.

What is your relationship to the Hermès archives—do you dip in regularly? When you go to the archives, there is a core of strong ideas: the perfect coat, the little leather jacket. I absorbed it fast. But they don't "haunt" me at all—*au contraire*. They're like Ali Baba's cave. You always fall on something with a layer of delicate imagination, which is not something we necessarily associate with Hermès.

Some of Hermès' designs, like the smiley-faced Mangeoire bag, are so unexpected and funny. Have you intentionally tried to mix things up? When you design you are not imposing, you are influencing. There are definitely some strong stereotypes about Hermès, which are not created by the house. But the house is alive—what I want to reveal with my work is its modernity through my collections.

How does the equestrian history fit into your design thinking? I have a strong personal connection to nature that is reflected in the AW18 collection. You can take on the equestrian influences in a traditional way and really indulge in gorgeous double-faced cashmere, or you can do it in a modern way, where you use technical fabrics and develop clothes that relate to the spirit of the outdoors with strong, functional outerwear.

The fashion community is very international, but Hermès' French heritage is clearly quite important. How do you balance those two things? There is definitely something French about it because we work with French artisans; you can recognize a certain style. Thirty, forty years ago, it was easy to look at someone and say "Oh, you're from here," but today the borders are blending.

Do you like the rhythm of fashion? The industry shifts so quickly. This is happening everywhere. If you look, how many art fairs are there a year? How many movies do you see? You open Netflix and you see 6,000 new series. The creative rhythm has been accelerated. Writers need to finish a book in two months because they have to launch it before the holidays because that's the best time… It asks too much. I'm living it, and always have. I do four strong collections a year. But when you're a creative person, you have to learn to react quickly.

What are some non-fashion references that have influenced your aesthetic? It's strange, the creative process. I often think about the artist Josef Albers and his approach at Black Mountain College. It was about how you educate a soul: through listening to music, studying architecture… he was really broad. I'm not into stereotypes, but I'm also not afraid of bad taste.

Do you have any art practices on the side? Lately, I have developed a really strong connection with my iPad [laughs]. I collect a lot of images, and also draw with my finger.

Does fashion have a place in the ongoing conversation about female empowerment? I always laugh when people say "Oh, I should be feminine." What is that? Is it to show your *décolleté*? In each era, there was a way to dress to reflect femininity, and also to own the body. But we have to be careful, because feminism is actually very serious, and you don't want it to become too much of a trend. Fashion has been a weird weakness of feminism—it has both constrained and liberated women.

How have you adapted your style as you've moved between fashion houses? I look at a *maison* as a person. You have to understand its psychology. At Céline, with Phoebe Philo, it was about being extremely radical: How can we have a strong color-silhouette identity? At The Row, the job was to really reveal the vision of Mary-Kate and Ashley [Olsen], creating this American elegance. With Hermès, I want it to arouse a dream, but somehow be approachable.

It's hard to do both! It is—it's a bit contradictory. For instance, when I arrived, [shoe designer] Pierre Hardy said: "Why not do trainers for the second show?" So we did a swimsuit with trainers. It's about bringing a more casual vocabulary to a silhouette, just loosening up the wardrobe a little bit.

As the designer, do you imagine yourself as a hypothetical user? There are designers who say, "I would never wear this." I try to imagine different morphologies: for a petite woman, a rounder woman. I try to be comprehensive. It's almost like being a filmmaker and having all your characters.

"I always laugh when people say 'Oh, I should be feminine.'
What is that? Is it to show your décolleté?"

The designer is drawn to abstraction, as evidenced by her love of artists such as František Kupka.

Archive:
Martha Gellhorn

In her 20s, *Martha Gellhorn* filed dispatches from the frontline of the Spanish Civil War. In her 80s,
she reported on the invasion of Panama. *Cody Delistraty* delves into the archives of one of the world's greatest war
correspondents—and explains why she succeeded despite, not because of, her famous husband.

In 1937, at the age of 29, Martha Gellhorn left for Madrid with a knapsack of clothes, a contract with *Collier's* magazine to write about the Spanish Civil War and little else. She had $50 in her pocket and no bank account. This was to be her break free.

Born in St. Louis, Gellhorn had graduated from the all-women's Bryn Mawr College in a tony Philadelphia suburb, placed a few articles in *The New Republic* and signed on as a crime reporter at the *Albany Times Union* in upstate New York. She'd been raised in a particularly progressive manner—her father, a gynecologist, seeing that her biology class textbooks in high school blurred out the anatomically explicit parts, petitioned her school to have them made more accurate; her mother, an outspoken advocate of women's voting rights, took her to rallies like the Missouri Votes for Women Parade and eventually helped Missouri win the vote for women in 1920.

Gellhorn had already traveled widely, both abroad as a brochure-writer for a cruise ship company and as a student visiting Germany, as well as domestically, writing a series of dispatches from the Midwest on rural poverty after the Great Depression, as a part of the New Deal's media push. But she wanted to be everywhere, to know everything, especially when the reports coming out of Europe leading up to the Second World War seemed fishy, spoon-fed to wire reporters by the governments involved. "It seems to me that they feed war reporters at these ridiculous briefings in the ballroom of hotels miles from anywhere," she later wrote.

Just a year after arriving in Spain, Gellhorn found herself in the middle of the Spanish Civil War, evoking its bizarre, banal atmosphere for American readers. "In Barcelona, it was perfect bombing weather," she wrote in a November 1938 report. "The cafés

In the early 1930s, Gellhorn was invited to the White House by her friend Eleanor Roosevelt so she could talk directly to the president about her reporting on the unemployment crisis.

along the Ramblas were crowded. There was nothing much to drink; a sweet fizzy poison called orangeade and a horrible liquid supposed to be sherry. There was, of course, nothing to eat. Everyone was out enjoying the cold afternoon sunlight."

She met up with Ernest Hemingway, whom she'd run into at a bar near his summer home in Key West, Florida, a year earlier. In Spain, they became close, traveling and working together, eventually falling in love. But his manifold sexual and masculine insecurities, set against Gellhorn's quest for independence, combined to create the most confrontational of his four marriages and perhaps the trickiest psychological situation of Gellhorn's life.

After they left Europe, married and briefly settled in Cuba, Gellhorn got cabin fever and returned to Europe to cover the Normandy invasion for *Collier's*. Hemingway followed. As the more famous writer of the two of them, he told the magazine he wanted her assignment—stealing it out from under her. But as he wrote about the invasion from afar, Gellhorn snuck onto a hospital ship that was returning to Omaha Beach to pick up wounded Allied soldiers, a risky move that allowed her to write a more intimate and compelling account of the invasion—one that sold far better and was read far wider than Hemingway's article.

Hemingway was irked, his masculinity challenged again, and a year later, after a fight at the posh Dorchester Hotel in London, she walked out on him —a husband who consistently tried to scuttle her career in order to bolster his own. Gellhorn was perhaps the greatest investigative reporter of the 20th century. She was, to put it simply, everywhere: at the Nuremberg Trials, at Russia's war against Finland, at the Vietnam War, in the Palestine

"'Why should I be a footnote to somebody else's life?' she famously asked."

Philip Kaufman's 2012 biopic about the Gellhorn-Hemmingway romance, which starred Nicole Kidman and Clive Owen, was poorly received. "[Kidman] works hard on the ambitious, intrepid Gellhorn but makes her seem smaller than life," wrote *The New York Times*.

refugee camps, at the McCarthy hearings, amid the Nicaraguan contras, even, at the age of 81, at the invasion of Panama. But her intensity as a globe-trekking journalist and the fact that she was a woman—and a well-dressed and typically feminine one at that—often conspired against her.

Conventionally, there have been two ways to view Gellhorn, both of which cut along gendered lines: as a fashionable femme fatale—a blond using her sex and her savvy to get stories that her male counterparts could never reach—or as a brassy, hardworking woman who chain-smoked and drank hard, forever poking at her sticky typewriter. That is, either a seductress or a shrew.

But Gellhorn is harder to categorize than that. She found that putting too much emphasis on her gender was not empowering but rather harmful, even calling out feminists whose insistence on female power, she believed, tended to end up as more condescending than enabling. "Feminists nark me," she wrote. "I think they've done a terrible disservice to women, branding us as 'women's writers.' Nobody says men writers; before, we were all simply writers."

She has also long been accused of using her sexuality in unethical ways. "She knew how important sex was for most men, and she used it not only to please men but to get good stories," wrote the biographer Carl Rollyson, whose

reporting and analysis have been widely disputed, including by Gellhorn herself, who wrote him a 25-page rebuttal upon reading his draft of *Beautiful Exile: The Life of Martha Gellhorn*. "She slept with generals; she had one-night stands with ordinary soldiers who might not survive the next day," Rollyson added, undeterred. "She dressed elegantly, used makeup skillfully, flirted, and coaxed men to do her bidding."

And yet, as much as she supposedly leveraged sex for her job, she also never much liked it. "If I practiced sex out of moral conviction, that was one thing; but to enjoy it... seemed a defeat," she wrote as a more reflective 64-year-old. "All I got was a pleasure of being wanted, I suppose, and the tenderness (not nearly enough) that a man gives when he is satisfied. I daresay I was the worst bed partner in five continents."

Gellhorn was a feminist in deeds, despite her dislike of any obsession with gender; she was a woman who rarely found sexual connections but who also slept around. She was a bundle of paradoxes. "On the one hand, she saw no need for the help of feminism in any shape or form, saying that she had never been discriminated against in any way," Caroline Moorehead, Gellhorn's major biographer and the collector of her letters, told me. "On the other, she made the most of her looks and charm, knew she pleased men,

used that fact to get to places and do things she wouldn't have been able to do otherwise."

But even more than a condescending kind of feminism, even more than accusations that she slept with anyone and everyone who might be a potential source, what Gellhorn hated most was being in another's shadow, especially Hemingway's. "Why should I be a footnote to somebody else's life?" she famously asked. She wrote five novels over her lifetime, two of which she published before even meeting Hemingway. (She also wrote 14 novellas and two collections of short stories.)

"I feel Martha is still grappling with the patriarchy in death," Iona Craig, a British investigative journalist who's won the Orwell Prize for Journalism and the Martha Gellhorn Prize for Journalism, told me. "Women have made considerable progress since Martha led the way in reporting on conflict. The large number of female reporters now regularly covering wars around the world is a significant part of Martha's legacy. When we can remember Martha for that rather than as 'the wife of...' then we'll know we've made greater strides forward."

In her final years, living in a sixth-floor apartment on Cadogan Square in London, Gellhorn hosted a variety of distinguished friends, including many authors and war reporters. Her only rule was that no one speak of

Hemingway. Even after a relatively brief, five-year marriage, he was still a central point of conversation.

It is indeed unfair to assign too great a significance to Hemingway's time in her life, but he is nonetheless instructive in understanding how she ended up thinking of herself as both a woman and a journalist. Like Pablo Picasso or a number of other male "geniuses," he afflicted the women in his life in a psychosexual way, attempting to leverage his fame and power within his relationships. When Gellhorn later wrote, "A man must be a very great genius to make up for being such a loathsome human being," her implication was that Hemingway was at once a loathsome human being and perhaps not a very great genius after all. But it didn't much matter to

her. Her combination of a beautiful, traditionally feminine exterior with an ambition and drive that was, at the time, considered traditionally masculine ultimately led Hemingway to trouble. Unable to control her and seeing his own failings mirrored back—as when she outdid him in covering D-Day—he tried to take control of their relationship with ever more brazen power grabs. But Gellhorn wouldn't have it. She wouldn't play his psychosexual game.

Gellhorn extracted herself altogether from questions of gender—embodying both what might be considered feminine and masculine. There was little difference as far as she cared; what she wanted was a great story, to hold the global hegemons accountable. Before she

died—swallowing a cyanide capsule in bed—she got into a silk slip and began going about her London apartment organizing documents and contracts, calling friends, sorting out who she'd give her jewelry to. It was February 15, 1998, and she was 89. She was half blind from a botched cataracts operation and dying from ovarian cancer that was spreading to her liver.

"I have never found what I was seeking and probably never will," she wrote in one of her final letters. But Gellhorn also likely saw that her dismissal of gender stereotypes—and her independence in just about every facet of her life—had freed her from mundaneness that plagues so many others.

"I've had a wonderful life," she added. "I didn't deserve it but I've had it."

Gellhorn fictionalized her life as a war correspondent. In *A Stricken Field* (1940), her protagonist Mary wrestles with questions of journalistic integrity in wartime Prague.

3

Hospitality

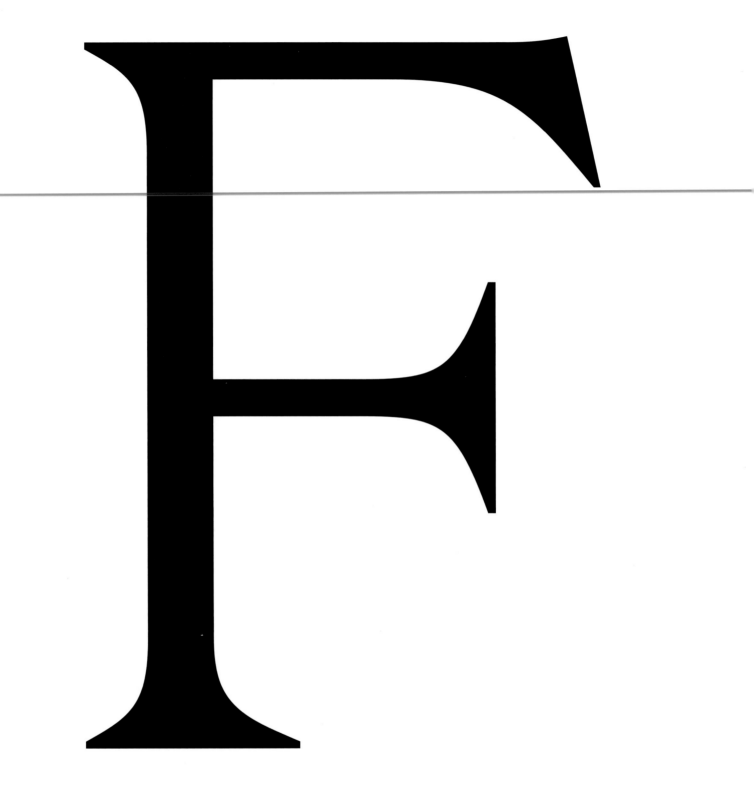

Flynn McGarry speaks with the judicious maturity that you'd expect from a person who's worked in kitchens for half of his life. That's because, despite being only 20, he has. McGarry has been cooking since the age of 10—first at dinner parties for his parents' friends, then at supper clubs hosted at their house in California's San Fernando Valley, then with apprenticeships at three-starred Michelin restaurants including Geranium in Copenhagen, Alinea in Chicago and Maaemo in Oslo. He opened a pop-up restaurant, Eureka, at the age of 13. McGarry has brought a playful joie de vivre into the often hyper-controlled environment of the professional kitchen, opening up his menus to spur-of-the-moment ideas without compromising on what's most important to the young chef: creating a meal that makes his guests, and himself, feel right at home. Having opened the doors to his own restaurant—Gem—on New York's Lower East Side in February 2018, McGarry is ready to shake off the distraction of the "teen chef" label and get on with doing the only thing he's ever really wanted to do: cook.

"I was cooking dishes from the books but they tasted different. I wanted to have fun."

Was food a big thing in your home growing up? Weirdly, it was never something that we spoke about. My parents made sure to get nice ingredients and food was always there but it didn't go any further than that. I think that's partially why I gravitated so much toward it, wanting to have something that was my own. Fine dining was truly new and unexplored to me then, different from everything else that I'd known up until that point.

Do you remember your first encounter with cooking? When I was 10, I was home from school sick and passing time watching food shows. I essentially had a lot of free time and wanted to try it out. There was no intentional notion of "I need to learn how to cook now"—it was something that I was simply into at the time. I quickly grew more interested in it and wanted to get a cookbook, so my mom took me to a bookstore. Like any child that wants the fancy toy, I eyed one on the top shelf— nicely wrapped and everything. It happened to be *The French Laundry Cookbook* by Thomas Keller. That book was what initially exposed me to fine dining, shifting my perspective on cooking from "making dinner" to more of an art form in itself. Looking at the dishes in the book was akin to hearing an incredible song that you can't truly grasp—you're intuitively drawn toward it though clueless as to how you'd perform it.

What part did the increasing popularity of supper clubs play in your early success? The supper clubs allowed me, as a young kid, to do my own thing—they're a way of showing and exploring what you can do without committing to having a restaurant. It didn't start as a public venture, nor with the intention of people actually having to make reservations—it was literally me on my days off from school, cooking for my parents' friends because I wanted to. You can be one of the best chefs ever, but if there isn't anyone around to eat your food, it doesn't really matter.

Did the internet help? You had a large online following from a young age. It's been great for me, helping pull back some of the mystery behind "that kid who's doing fine dining." On the flip side, I think it makes you become more of an idea—it propelled the whole "teen chef" label more than would've been the case had I not been featured so heavily online. At the end of the day, and especially in this industry, anything that gets people interested in what you do is probably worth doing.

Do you remember the first dish that you cooked for someone? I remember the first dinner that I did at my family's house. I was 11 years old and had friends from school helping me out. The guests were my parents' friends. It was a five-course menu—truly just me trying out recipes from the French Laundry and Alinea cookbooks. I was cooking dishes from the books but they looked and tasted different. I wanted to have more fun, adding a bit of grit. I think that still shines through to this day—being inspired by these perfect versions of restaurants yet adding a more youthful and crude energy. I learned very quickly that I loved many aspects of fine-dining restaurants but there were some things that I didn't like. I realized that the dishes that are perfectly cut and manicured were the opposite of what I wanted to do—I didn't want to spend hours cutting a vegetable into perfect little cubes. I've never been attracted to restaurants that show how much time they've spent on things through the neatness of a dish.

Do you think food is shaped by nostalgia? Nostalgia comes into any creative act, whether you realize it or not. A lot of the dishes that I do are, often unknowingly, shaped by some type of memory. I can look at something that I made a year ago and remember an incident that happened that week which inspired me to wake up and put these-and-those ingredients together. When I look at the dishes that we make at the restaurant, they aren't ingredients on a plate; they're rather an experience or emotion that I've had. It's an interesting thing to replicate on a nightly basis yet that's where you need that slightly rustic sentiment too—we can make a course perfect but there's something more emotional about the food when your approach is somewhat unhinged. Sure, it might not be as pretty as a dish that took hours to perfect, but what you're eating gives you the feeling of a person having cooked for you in their home. The nights that I remember the most are those spent at a friend's house for dinner and hanging out for the whole night—it's that emotion that I want to bring to our guests.

Previous spread: McGarry wears a sweater by Todd Snyder. Left: He wears a sweater by Todd Snyder and a coat by Mr. P. Above: He wears a shirt by Billy Reid, trousers by Todd Snyder and boots by Allen Edmonds.

How do you see the difference between cooking for paying customers and cooking for friends and family? We realized at Gem that we'd essentially be serving 36 strangers a night. It boils down to presenting ourselves in an unapologetic and humble way, being transparent from the second people walk through the door. Gem is not a restaurant where you pick what you want from the menu; you visit us for something that is curated by a single person—from the food, to the flowers, to the interior, to the wine. It's different from other places, but those who come here understand it. Even when they're ordering wine, they ask: "What do you recommend?" It's this beauty of not presenting a menu in advance and instead having people who are open-minded about what you have prepared for them. That's what a dinner party essentially is—going to someone's house to hang out and drink and eat whatever they've made for you.

It seems that intuition plays an important part in keeping things personal. Spontaneity has always been present at the best restaurants that I've been to—this feeling of things being thrown together, just people cooking a nice meal for you. I sometimes think that going to a fast-food restaurant is similar to a fine-dining restaurant—everything has been meticulously figured out to the last minuscule detail with no room for expression. Nothing's perfect when you have friends and family over for dinner and everything's a bit more rustic and personal—you just want it to taste good. It's a constant struggle to hit the balance of things being homemade and delicious while also being very elegant and beautiful in their simplicity.

You deviated from the traditional path of most chefs who spend years working their way up in the kitchens of others before setting out on their own. Were you ever nervous about making that choice? Everything that's happened since I started cooking has felt like a natural progression, doing things when they felt right. With Gem, everything fell into place—the timing with the space becoming available and people being willing to invest. I could have probably taken a less stressful and daunting route but it seemed like if there ever was a time to do it, now was it. I've always been aware that Gem could totally not work out and

if so, that's fine. There will always be a point within the lifespan of an idea where it won't float anymore, and at that point I'll do something else. That's also what's so great about doing this at my age: The restaurant could fail tomorrow and I would still have many, many years to figure out what I'd want to do next. If I postponed opening up my own place until I was 35 years old only to fail then, there would be a lot more on the line.

In the documentary about you, *Chef Flynn*, you say: "I had 10 years of childhood and that was enough." Are you ever afraid of one day looking back and feeling that you missed out on certain things because you spent so much time cooking? I reached a point at an early age where I didn't want to just hang out anymore. Honestly, I've spent my time doing exactly what I wanted to do—I even have the privilege of being able to choose not to, if that was what I wanted. I understand that very few people have that kind of luxury and I'm in a lucky place, being able to do so. I can't do things unless I feel comfortable with them, especially on a creative level. It was the same going to school—I was literally incapable of going there every day. I was fortunate to have supportive parents who let me do things my own way and doing so from the outset has led to me having no actual regrets looking back.

You're about to turn 20. The "teen chef" label will be gone. Are there any aspects of being a young person within a grown-up industry that you'll miss? No. I hope that it'll be a nice way to turn a new leaf in my career. Being young can open a lot of doors until you reach a point where you're left alone to figure it all out. It's time to challenge the idea that the time you've spent doing something is equal to how skilled you are. To me, it has very much been about showing that you can spend five years doing something—figuring out how to do it well—and then do it 10 times better than someone who's been doing it for 20 years.

What do you imagine it'll be like to be considered a chef—full stop? To be thought of, and judged, at the same level as any other chef is all that I've ever wanted. There's an extra amount of pressure now but I definitely welcome it. I'm ready.

"Going to a fast-food restaurant is similar to a fine-dining restaurant—everything has been meticulously figured out with no room for expression."

McGarry wears a sweater by Todd Snyder and a suit by Brooklyn Tailors.

Table

Swatch, sample and swap with abandon. Until the scissors come out, nothing's off the table.

Photography by *Christian Møller Andersen*

Textiles

Previous spread: Hermès. Left and above: Kvadrat. Overleaf left: Kvadrat. Overleaf right: Hermès. Page 126-127: Kvadrat

HOW TO AWARD

What sets a great host apart? We spent 24 hours trailing the professionals.

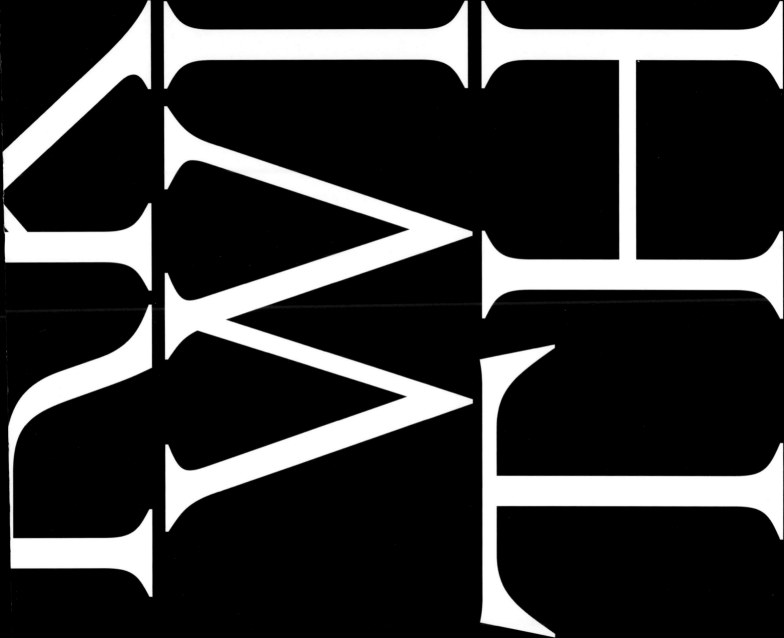

A Parisian café owner explains how to make the most of the calm before doors open at midday.

Morning:
Coralie Jouhier

Photography by
Jean-Marie Franceschi

Jouhier and her boyfriend Daqui Gomis named Jah Jah, their restaurant, after the Rastafari god Jah.

"We wanted a place that feels like our home," says Coralie Jouhier, the co-owner of Afro-Caribbean vegan café Jah Jah by Le Tricycle. Her approach to vegan fare—and the space in which she serves it—dispels any stale stereotypes that might cling to ethical eating. "A lot of people thought vegan food was only eating salad or that it was a 'white' thing," says Jouhier, whose mother and father hail from Martinique and Senegal respectively and raised her on a diet rich in fruit and vegetables.

Jouhier sees Jah Jah as a natural way of sharing her multicultural heritage with fellow Parisians while encouraging a broader understanding of animal-free cooking. "It's important to respect your culture and share it in the most beautiful way you can, with a lot of love, so that people can learn about it," she says.

Since expanding the business from a hot dog cart to a brick-and-mortar café with her boyfriend and business partner Daqui Gomis, the former model has sought to create a warm, ecletic space in which her customers can experience her philosophy toward food. The bold

red, yellow and green colors of the Rastafari flag decorate the walls; a framed print of the African continent sits amid souvenirs collected on far-flung travels. Glance at the menu and names like Le Dogtor Dre (a vegan hot dog) reveal some of Jouhier's hip-hop heroes, while an Instagram feed advertises reggae parties and in-store yoga. "It's a very personal restaurant," she says. "We really want to share and discover with different kinds of people."

With the lunchtime rush looming each day, mornings are an integral period for preparation and experimentation at Jah Jah. Jouhier—who wakes up early to stretch, gulp down some water and mentally run through her to-do list for the day—uses this quiet time to cook and also to teach new recipes to her team in the kitchen. By the time patrons begin to trickle through the door, she has snuck out again, returning home to spend time with her baby daughter.

As a young restaurateur in a city saturated with exceptional places to eat, Jouhier has always relied on one key ingredient: conviction.

Afternoon:
Chris Glass

For Chris Glass, the responsibilities of hospitality are best captured by a German word: *aufgabe*. Roughly translating as "a task," it reflects the dedication that has seen Atlanta-born Glass establish a reputation in Berlin as a consummate master of ceremonies. "The energy—the intention of wanting to connect people—is a line that runs through everything that we do," he says of his latest venture, APTM, a loft apartment complete with corner kitchen and bedroom that serves as an intimate space in which to host functions, food and drink tastings and Glass' annual Thanksgiving meal. Combining flamboyant, design-led pieces with the functionality of a private home, APTM (or A Place to Meet) encourages daytime meetings to take

a less conservative tone and evening events to progress into bona fide parties. Here, Glass explains why mixing business with pleasure should be done more often.

It's a novel concept to design an event space that looks like a home. Does it reflect the changing nature of how we do business? When things are politically sensitive, we see a desire to return to environments that are safe and nurturing. I think a home is the ultimate example of that. People have jobs that allow them flexibility and a nomadic lifestyle. So, to blend what would typically be a work environment and a home environment has given way to spaces that are comfortable but functional at the same time.

Can a particular environment set the tone for a meeting? When it's a comfortable and personal environment that's inviting and warm, then people are much more likely to let their hair down. We often say the best parties begin and end in the kitchen. When people feel like they can take their shoes off and cozy up to the countertop, then layers of themselves come out that they're not necessarily used to showing. At the end of the day, it's the biggest compliment to the host that people feel at home.

When in an environment that serves multiple purposes, how can a group of people transition from work to fun? Most people would probably look for really clear triggers: taking

A modern master of ceremonies charts the decline of formal meetings, and shares the secret of "The Squeeze."

Photography by *Dennis Weber*

Glass opened event space APTM last year in a 1905 carriage house in Berlin's Wedding neighborhood.

a jacket or tie off, having a drink. But because entertaining is a big part of how I live my life, both professionally and personally, I feel like I'm a step beyond that already. I've gone back to really trying to find the way to make these two [sides] as synced up as possible versus trying to make one different than the other. I know that people are looking for a person at the table—whether that's a meeting table or a dinner table—instead of a robot.

As someone who entertains for a living, what are your tricks for establishing a connection with guests from different industries or cultures? "The Squeeze" started as a habit and became a custom. At some point between courses,

I get up, make my way around the table, and gently put my hand on the shoulder of each guest to connect with them. It's a great opportunity for me to introduce them to someone that I think they should know or to make sure their meal was what they wanted.

How do you draw a meeting to a close? When I was growing up, my mom had the ability to speak volumes without ever opening her mouth. She'd simply look at you and be really distinct about what she wanted to communicate with her eyes. I think you can help people understand that it's time to wrap up by looking at them very intently and smiling slightly. It always worked for my mom.

Photography by
Dan Smith

Charlotte Wilde knows the pleasurable sway that wine can exert over an evening. She established her credentials as a founding member of East London hot spot Sager + Wilde and with her latest venture—a multipurpose creative space called Darling—she is continuing to influence how we consume fine wine. Here, Wilde shares her secrets for hosting a gathering that hits all the right notes.

What are the basic requirements for hosting a successful drinks party? It's important to have excellent glassware and to make sure that the wines are at the right temperature. And it's nice before people arrive to open all the bottles and taste them to make sure they're in good condition. Often wines need to be decanted a couple of hours before, so it's good to get that done in advance so that everything's ready to go.

Are there any unnecessary extras that can be avoided? There's a trend at the moment for people to use these at-home cooling machines and gadgets. I think all of that is unnecessary. I personally like the idea of taking a white wine out of the fridge, pouring it out, and then just putting it on the table. I don't think it necessarily needs to stay at that temperature. In fact, I like when it's warmed up a little bit. I also think too much glassware on the table is overwhelming.

How does your experience in the hospitality business translate to home gatherings? Hospitality is about being mindful and paying attention to detail, whether that's remembering to take someone's coat or making sure to offer them a drink. If you're a good host then you can be a good host in a wine bar, you can be a good host in somebody else's house and you can certainly be a great host in your own home.

Which details encourage the right ambience at evening drinks? I'm quite a homebody so I'm all about setting the mood. I work very hard to make it look effortless; I love to have linen napkins and the glassware is super important. I also like neutral colors—I find it quite calming, especially in a dining environment—so I'll incorporate lots of natural earth tones. It's about simplicity, but also showing that you've made an effort.

Are there any golden rules for wine tasting? A lot of people get confused when someone brings over a bottle of wine and asks you to try it. You don't actually need to taste it—most of the time, they're not asking to see if you like it, they're asking you to see if the wine is in good condition. All you need to do is smell it.

Can different wines create different moods? Wine can be very emotive. It's led by seasons and trend, with certain wines that people drink for certain occasions. It's also geographical— you'll probably drink one type of wine if you're on holiday in a warm climate and another type of wine if you're in London in December. When I talk to people about wine, a lot of the time I won't use descriptors because I don't associate wine characteristics with words like "fruity" or "minerality." Instead, I'll talk about where I was when I drank it as that, for me, is a more evocative and interesting way to create a memory and a mood.

What do we gain from drinking together? Wine is one of the most hedonistic things that you can ever really experience in life. I love the fact that it starts a conversation. It's amazing to learn other people's thoughts on a particular wine and I love listening to their narratives and vocabulary when they're talking about it.

Evening:
Charlotte Wilde

A wine bar doyenne instructs on how to throw a party fit for Bacchus in your own home.

Meet the Parisian hotelier who spends sleepless nights
ensuring that his guests have the opposite.

Night:
Adrien Gloaguen

Photography by *Jean-Marie Franceschi*

Adrien Gloaguen, the independent hotelier behind three of Paris' most sought-after boutique hotels, knows that his reputation rests on whether his guests feel at home. In an industry that revolves around single-night stays in anonymous suites, he deliberately fosters a culture of warmth and familiarity. Each of his hotels boasts its own spin on creature comforts: from the snug reading room at Hôtel Paradis equipped with books and magazines to the little chocolates from the capital's oldest chocolate factory found in the rooms of Hotel Panache.

Service is approached with the same consideration. "We are not five-star hotels, but each general manager knows their clients really well and tries to give each of them attention," says Gloaguen. For some, that might mean their favorite cake waiting for them at breakfast. For others, it's the concierge helping with trip arrangements or misplaced luggage. Gloaguen recalls one guest arriving frazzled and frustrated after the airline had lost their bags—his team kicked into action and, two days later, the suitcases were delivered to their door. "But the most important thing is to smile," he says. "The big trick—the most important but the hardest—is to be kind. I incentivize each employee to give their best attention to the guest."

It helps that he seems to like most of the people that pass through his hotels' doors. In general, he says, patrons abide by the well-worn maxim of treating the hotel like they would their home—in a good way. "In 95 percent of cases, I don't have to be strict with our clients," he says. Occasionally, a room is left wrecked or a guest tries to barter their breakfast in exchange for a favorable TripAdvisor review. When the latter situation crops up, Gloaguen is quick to shut them down: "We say no."

After more than a decade of professional hosting, Gloaguen is inching ever closer to nailing the perfect night's sleep. The first part, he says, is getting each bedroom's basics exactly right. "The hospitality business is so focused on decor and marketing that sometimes we forget the most important thing in a hotel: to have a good night's sleep." With that in mind, he always invests in excellent mattresses and paints the walls in delicate, restful shades. The second component requires greater effort but the payoff as a host is deeply rewarding. "It's the most wonderful experience to erase the problems of your clients," he says. "Each small thing that we can do to liberate their mind is the best way for them to have a great sleep."

Gloaguen opened his first hotel, Paradis, at the age of 25. His very first guest was British rapper M.I.A.

THE INHOSPITABLE CITY

TEXT:
HUGO MACDONALD

The public square is to the city as the living room is to the home: a place of welcome, and in which to gather. But these spaces are under threat. They are being shrunk and sold off by politicians, and abandoned by individuals in favor of their virtual alternatives. Hugo Macdonald considers what we have to lose.

It is an uncomfortable fact that the social contact our public spaces once gave us is no longer beyond our front door but at our fingertips. The town square is now social media, the park bench is the comment thread, the picnic blanket is the WhatsApp group. Glance around any city and you'll see more people engrossed in their virtual lives than engaged in the public realm before them.

What happens when virtual space is a more compelling refuge than public space? What then for our urban experience and quality of life? Public space is and always has been a vital part of the city. From the temple to the forum, the piazza to the park, for as long as cities have existed, the need for citizens to gather together (and alone) in public has been recognized and accommodated as a basic right. Beyond the confines of the home and the workplace, public space is what determines our urban experience. It's not just a social nicety, but a necessity. It significantly shapes the physical and mental quality of life of a city's inhabitants. Yet today, the very notion of public space is in flux, diminishing rapidly in scale and alarmingly in generosity. We seem to be forgetting how to use it as a real platform, whether for social engagement or solo disengagement.

New York–trained, London-based clinical psychologist Dr. Siri Harrison is on the front line—dealing with mental health issues relating to the consequences of this shift. "Living in dense urban populations creates common problems," she explains. "It increases our sense of anonymity, which can heighten feelings of loneliness when we need a sense of community to thrive; it increases our sense of competition with others, so instead of diving into doing what we do well, we become fixated with winning over someone else; and, taken together, these issues lead to plummeting self-esteem. We delve into 'false refuges' for comfort such as overworking or drinking too much. It is a depressive and anxious existence, which can become a vicious cycle."

Harrison doesn't prescribe public space as a cure, so much as acknowledge its importance in helping us to flourish in an inherently abnormal, unnatural habitat: "Public space is crucial to human well-being. We are social animals and we need others." She says that we need time, space and other people in our downtime given the fast pace of urban life: "We need to relearn the art of 'being' and not always 'doing' to achieve and attain more. Good public spaces in the city provide much-needed physical and mental space for us to reconnect with what truly matters and nourish our quality of life."

Our changing relationship with public space is personal and also political. Public space is increasingly becoming private and, although private land can be beautifully designed, pro-grammed and maintained, we are only welcome due to the benevolence of its owners. Areas where we used to be free to do whatever we wished, from eating a sandwich to staging a protest, suddenly have rules and regulations; rather than serving public interest, they serve the interests of private owners. Dr. Bradley Garrett, a social and cultural geography professor at the University of Sydney, is also a "place hacker," crusading for greater transparency in the boundaries between public and private space, and greater rights for the public in the latter. "Privatization of public spaces happens for three reasons," he explains. "Simple economics—local authorities strapped for cash hand over the maintenance of public space to save money; liability today is an important factor—risk averse councils don't want to be held responsible for accidents or anything they might be held accountable for; most sinister though is the governmental policy of selling off public land by way of controlling the population. If the government is in charge, people have democratic rights. If land is privately owned, then the owner has total rights."

Garrett acknowledges that privatized public land looks and works for most people in the same way as public space. But he points out, "You will notice when you want to have a beer, run your dog or stage a protest." Private-public space is governed by rules, more often than not monitored by CCTV and patrolled by security guards. Rules can be buried in small print on a website, but security enforcement is not so subtle. "It's threatening," Garrett says. "We are at the whim of a single individual to enforce whatever they don't like. Most people shrink when confronted by an authority figure; not many question where the rule is or why it's in place." While it's fine to eat a sandwich on a bench in privately owned public space, it's not okay to protest. "It matters when people take to the streets," Garrett continues. "Access to public space is fundamental to democracy. Privatizing public space allows authorities to kettle marches and protests. It is a very effective form of control."

Whether public or private, design has been used as a way to curb antisocial behavior for centuries. The Georgians installed iron railings with decorative spikes to delineate private from public areas in London. The Victorians designed ingenious slanted stone urine deflectors for street corners to stop men relieving themselves in public. The introduction of gas street lighting was intended as a deterrent for more serious criminals.

Today, we would call this "hostile design"—a method of controlling who does what and where—that has become more virulent over time. Cities now install spikes on surfaces to prevent people sitting down, immovable armrests on benches to stop people lying down, awkwardly shaped furniture to ensure they don't stay too long and invisible grease to prevent rogue wall climbers (or even leaners). The

absence of garbage cans forces us to move on in search of somewhere to deposit trash. Music that doesn't chime with a prevailing mood deliberately jars, like classical music playing in a place that could attract skateboarders. Lighting either doesn't exist, to engender a feeling of fear and move us on, or is purposely bright to ensure the same result—like lights-up at closing time.

Hostile design has quickly developed from a subgenre of Instagrammable "design fails" into a growing body of critical theory, determining ways in which our presence and behavior in public are controlled. The Victorians introduced these urban elements to prevent anti-social behavior, but hostile design today prevents social behavior too. The owners of privatized public spaces are free to draw the line on what they deem antisocial: skateboarders, buskers, homeless people, teenagers, dogs. Far from being the glue that holds a city's population together, life between buildings is characterized by corporate NIMBYism.

Public spaces decorated with uncomfortable concrete monoliths and spikes, patrolled by state or private security, don't have a positive atmosphere. Security guards don't automatically make people feel secure: At best, they serve to remind us of the threats we'd rather not live under, at worst, they institutionalize a sense of fear. The effect of constant monitoring is a siege mentality; the city at large quickly becomes an inhospitable environment. Arguably, it's little wonder we seek comfort in virtual worlds where we can curate our realities. They give us a semblance of control, which se-

duces and distracts us in equal measure. But at what cost in the real world?

"Cities are thoroughly physical places," wrote Jane Jacobs in her seminal 1961 treatise on human-centered urbanism, *The Death and Life of Great American Cities*. "In seeking understanding of their behavior, we get useful information by observing what occurs tangibly and physically, instead of sailing off on metaphysical fancies." Her words were aimed at planners, whose approach to public space was fanciful—marking out space on a city model rather than working it out in reality on the ground. But her point is more prescient today than ever: The best examples of effective public space are not counted off as requisite square feet in boardrooms but are responses to reality. Local markets and community gardens, children's play areas and outdoor swimming pools are enduringly successful pockets of life and activity because they both service and appeal to fundamentals of community needs and human desires. When people feel invested in their own public spaces, they feel alive.

Bas Losekoot is a Dutch photographer exploring the intersection of urbanism and psychology. He has recently completed a decade-long study called *The Urban Millennium Project*, photographing commuters in 10 cities around the world. His reportage portraits are arresting for their hyperrealism—he makes commuters look like movie stars. But they are memorable for the disarming expressions Losekoot captures in the faces of his unsuspecting subjects. Whether in New York or Mumbai,

"Cities now install spikes on surfaces to prevent people sitting down, immovable armrests on benches to stop people lying down and awkwardly shaped furniture to ensure they don't stay too long."

Lagos or Seoul, the expressions are similar: A thin veil of resilience masks an almost primal anguish. The strangers share a common gaze, with head lowered and body leaning forward. It is uncomfortable to look at these faces; Harrison's prognosis of our anxious existence is writ large in every frame. They appear simultaneously haunted and hunted—a perfect advertisement for moving to the countryside.

"I'm interested in capturing private lives in public places," Losekoot explains. "There's such a gulf between the physical and psychological proximity in how we live in cities. It's like we are wearing masks in public, as if we are all actors. There's a choreography in how people move around each other in this state. It's like an awkward dance." In his photographs, it seems like everyone is trying to hold onto themselves. As a documentation of urban humanity it is simultaneously beautiful and unsettling.

In the faces of Losekoot's subjects you feel the inhospitable city keenly. "The street is a pressure cooker for human expression," he says. One wonders what Jane Jacobs would make of this source material. Though city planners and private developers frequently pay her and her theories lip service, talking openly about the importance of public space for public health, rarely do they properly provide for a population that desperately needs a collective valve to release the pressures of contemporary urban life. The street, the park, the square and the church were historically opportunities for overcoming our collective anonymity. Today it is events rather than spaces that break

the impasse: the royal wedding, the World Cup, terror attacks.

As Garrett notes, public space today is driven by commercial needs more than social ones. "Human beings are habitual," he explains. "We get used to private enterprise in public space: tolls for entry, pop-up businesses that never pop down, weddings, concerts and so on." He is inherently mistrustful of commodified activities in public space: "We need spaces where things aren't being sold, or we are always customers." When public space is commercialized and programmed heavily it becomes too prescriptive. It feels restrictive, coercive and void of any serendipity. The governing sense is binary: This is what can and can't happen here. There is neither space nor trust left to imagine what might possibly happen.

In his book *Slow Burn City*, architecture critic Rowan Moore describes this stagnation: "The enemies of public space include the excess of vending, programming, branding and scripting, the things which, often but not always in the pursuit of profit, eliminate the spontaneous and uncalculated. There is a view of public space that defines its success by the number of people it attracts, and there are professional consultancies that employ quasi-scientific measures to assess it on these terms, which exalts to a dangerous degree quantity over quality. Sometimes you want some emptiness, too." Is it the responsibility of architects and designers to re-engage us with our urban public spaces? "Much of the time, the main task is to avoid designing out the possibilities of a place," writes

Moore. "A public space should enrich possibilities and expand freedoms."

As if in response, this year's architecture biennale in Venice, curated by Yvonne Farrell and Shelley McNamara of Irish practice Grafton Architects, took the title *Freespace*. Grafton's call to participate was accompanied by a manifesto, which explained their objective. It was to remind architects of the sense of humanity at the core of their agenda, and of their capacity to find additional and unexpected generosity in every project—even with the most private, defensive, exclusive or commercially restricted conditions.

"Freespace can be a space for opportunity, a democratic space, un-programmed and free for uses not yet conceived," they wrote. There were several examples in theory, process and practice, across projects of various scales and from various cultures. Recurring themes included the importance of emotion in architecture, and the capacity for materials and details to engage our senses. They remind us that architecture is inherently social and sociable—it brings people together to be the best of themselves. At a time when it's easy to feel demoralized by the inhospitable nature of our urban experience, here was a comprehensive response from the global architecture community that was human-centered, generous and, above all, optimistic. Grafton ended their manifesto with the Greek proverb, which should hang in every city hall and developer's boardroom: "A society grows great when old men plant trees whose shade they know they shall never sit in."

Home Tour:
Château de Gudanes

In 2013, an Australian couple bought a crumbling château in the French Pyrenees. Five years and innumerable power outages, leaks ând tears later, *Tristan Rutherford* discovers how a "naive willfulness" (and many eager volunteers) helped coax a ruin back to life. Photography by *Salva López* & Styling by *Cobalto Studio*

Château de Gudanes was built in the mid-18th century for wealthy nobleman Louis Gaspard de Sales, also known as "Le Roi des Pyrénées."

It was internet cookies that led Karina and Craig Waters to buy a 94-room château. The Australian couple's daughter, Jasmine, was on a school exchange in southwest France; as Craig followed her progress, his browser became inundated with property ads for the French Pyrenees. One pop-up featured the Château de Gudanes, a Dracula's castle-meets-*Downton Abbey* in the Aston Valley. The couple tacked it onto a tentative property viewing list for their forthcoming trip.

It was love at first sight, but there was just one problem: The Château de Gudanes was a forlorn wreck. It had neither water nor electricity, let alone a functioning roof. Trees grew from its turreted chimneys. Interior scaffolds were reflected in antique mirrors. Rooftop snowmelt dripped over Empire wallpaper dating from the late 1700s, back when when Voltaire and Diderot philosophized in the castle's principal salon. It was a house of horrors—an atrophied mansion with the power to give even the most accomplished accountant budgetary nightmares.

"The first time we saw the château we should have had more sense," says Karina, herself a chartered accountant. But she and Craig were enticed through the castle gates by its magic and charm. "Anyway, if we'd have thought about it too much we would never have embarked on the project." Karina describes her original vision as "very Australian. As in, you just get someone to fix up the place then we can play château!" Five years after the purchase in 2013, she concedes that "it didn't quite work out that way."

The Château de Gudanes' history is a tale of religious wars and ritzy pomp. In a storyline that puts *Game of Thrones* to shame, the protestant Gudanes barony was gifted to a son-in-law, stripped of assets during the French Revolution, auctioned by the state, pillaged during a peasant uprising, then re-purchased by the government for use as a children's summer camp in the 1970s.

The building's current incarnation was crafted by Ange-Jacques Gabriel, the go-to architect for King Louis XV of France. Gabriel used a similarly muscular grandeur for his Château du Petit Trianon at Versailles, which housed Louis' official mistress, Madame du Barry. By the 1990s, the Pyrenees château had fallen into such a state of disrepair that it was classified as a ruin and declared a *monument historique*. This official designation hindered relief efforts because any subsequent renovations had to be approved by the finicky regulations of France's Ministry of Culture.

This is where Karina's lack of local language skills or architectural knowledge came to the fore. A naive willfulness allowed her to find offbeat solutions where more experienced project managers would have failed. When it rained during the consolidation phase, she pitched a tent inside the château so she could carry on her travails. Her evolving Franglais insulated her from criticism, "because I couldn't understand what everybody was thinking." Karina claims that being a kindly Aussie rather than an invading Brit helped her cause. "Locals also understood the château's heritage and were embarrassed at how far it had fallen, so they had a heartfelt gratitude that someone was trying their best."

As the Waters family gave their all, the château gave up its secrets.

"You don't buy a château and think you'll live the same life."

In 2016, the Waters family was awarded a Medal of Honour by Prince Albert II of Monaco on behalf of the Institute of France in recognition of their efforts to restore the château.

"I try not to think more than three months ahead."

When the building team cleared 500 tons of rubble, they discovered Venetian glassware and faience pottery. They also found an eight-foot-wide tunnel bolted shut in the floor. Legend has it that during the religious conflicts that wracked southwest France, an escape tunnel ran from the château to the local village. "One of the counts apparently escaped by being put in a barrel, then rolled to safety," explains Karina. When the couple tried to excavate the shaft, however, "it was like we were digging all the way to Australia, so we temporarily stopped." Nevertheless, such discoveries blossomed into a narrative that inspired them to proceed.

After several months of restoration work, Karina's social media page had 50 likes from disbelieving family and friends. "Then one day I woke up and I thought the kids had hacked the site." One of Karina's blogs had been shared by HuffPost, pushing up the château's Facebook likes to 25,000. "Then my neighbor's 12-year-old daughter said I should get Instagram." After a slow start the feed was covered by a San Francisco newspaper. "Around 100,000 followers came on board in a few days," recalls Karina, who must have touched an earthy nerve for viewers glued to Silicon Valley screens. "Then all the accounts went up in big numbers and it hasn't stopped." The Château de Gudanes now offers a regular dose of pastoral bliss to 400,000 Facebook fans and more than 300,000 Instagram followers.

As if by magic, the derelict mansion became a fantasy castle where everyone wanted to stay. The château was now inundated not by leaks but by guests eager to help: Whispers of wildflowers and birdsong mingled with Neo-Latin and American-English, as curators, linguists and food foragers offered their services. Salon after salon was painstakingly excavated with the assistance of, for example, a team of Italian Byzantine fresco restorers. Work on the rear of the château revealed medieval friezes hidden under layers of plaster. Word of the restoration spread to an elderly gentleman whose family had owned the château from the 19th century until the 1950s. "The guy could see what had been accomplished was done with love and purpose." Both he and the Waterses shed tears.

As château guardian, Karina has the delicate job of channeling the resources of well-wishers. She created "Restore and Stay" packages for three, five and seven nights based on visitors' interests, ranging from yoga, to flea markets, to rock art and patisserie making. These paying volunteers engage in "château camping." Each is lodged in a semi-restored suite with a marble hearth and crumbling ceiling, rustically furnished with rococo bedsteads and dried flowers. A conservator from Britain's National Trust recently stayed, as did the NASA executive in charge of reconditioning the Apollo 13 spaceship, who passed on valuable restoration techniques. Dinner table conversations, fueled by local Ariège wine, are maelstroms of Languedocien linguistics and Mesozoic geology, of "kindred spirits and positive energy." Karina explains, "You don't buy a château and think you'll live the same life." Her accommodation is booked up until 2020.

Karina is a custodian of a rural idyll, rather than a strict mistress bossing staff at a boutique hotel, and she attributes her success to the laissez-faire character of her adopted country. "I love the way that the château is about what might happen. Long term? I try not to think more than three months ahead." Five years ago, she dove in at the deep end, and the castle has repaid her faith in spades. "After the château got all this publicity I received several publishing offers," she says. The result is a book that was published in September 2018. "It's titled *Château de Gudanes: A True Love Story Never Ends*, because love doesn't have a fairytale beginning. It's about hard work. About trust. And it's forever." The next chapter of the château's unlikely annals is just beginning.

When the Waterses bought the château, the roof had collapsed in four places and champagne buckets were deployed to catch rainwater.

CONCIERGE

L'HÔTEL

In Paris, chance encounters come knocking at the Hotel Plaza Athénée.

Left: Alexis wears socks by Falke, shoes by JM Weston and the uniform from Hotel Plaza Athénée, the storied, century-old hotel where Christian Dior showed his inaugural collection in 1947.

Suzie wears a dress by Dior, hat by Maison Michel, earrings by Raphaele Canot on White Bird, gloves by Isotoner, shoes by Gianvito Rossi and carries a bag and trunk by Louis Vuitton and a trunk by Mark Cross.

Suzie wears a dress by Rochas, hat by Laurence Bossion, earrings by Raphaele Canot on White Bird, scarf by Mulberry,
belt by Dior, gloves by Causse, bag by Edie Parker and shoes by A.P.C.

Suzie wears a shirt by Hermès, hat by Laurence Bossion and stylist's own earrings. Alexis wears a turtleneck sweater by De Fursac.

Above: Suzie wears a dress by Dior, turban by Laurence Bossion, earrings by Raphaele Canot on White Bird, vintage sunglasses by Chanel and carries a bag by Louis Vuitton. Alexis wears the Hotel Plaza Athénée uniform. Right: Suzie wears a polo shirt by Rochas, a scarf by Dior and vintage sunglasses by Chanel. Alexis wears a jacket by De Fursac and polo shirt by Charvet.

Alexis wears a suit by De Fursac and a shirt and bow tie by Charvet. Suzie wears a shirt by Hermès, a hat by Laurence Bossion and earrings by Raphaele Canot on White Bird.

Alexis wears a shirt by Brioni, trousers by HAKUÏ and socks by Falke.

Suzie wears a gown by Maticevski, earrings by Atelier Swarovski and turban by Laurence Bossion.

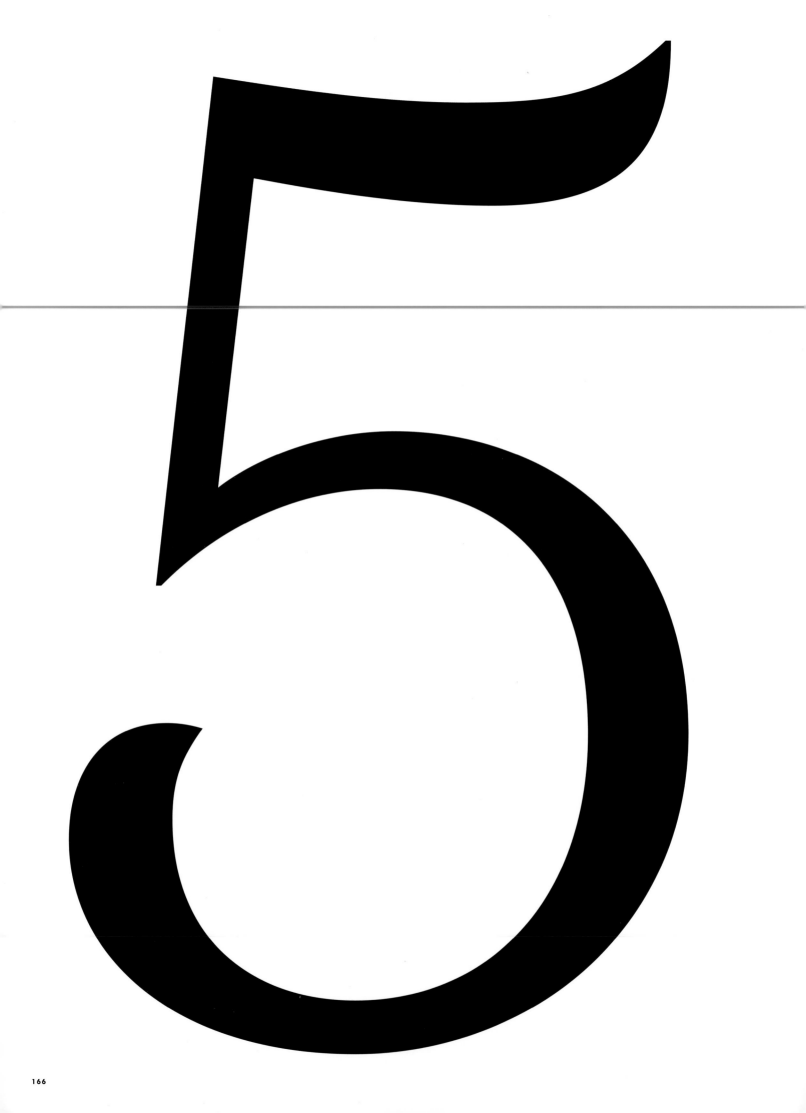

PILLARS
OF HOSTING

Photography by *Gustav Almestål* & Styling by *Andreas Frienholt*

HOW TO GO SOLO AT A PARTY — WORDS BY JUSTIN MYERS

Is it really better to arrive at a party in a group? It's certainly no guarantee of a conversation partner: Busy parties are often full of better offers and chances are you'll be left alone sooner or later. If you're a host, make sure to introduce guests as soon as they arrive. And if you're a guest flying solo, head straight for the kitchen and make a chatty inquiry about mixers, cocktail recipes or, if there's someone doing the playlist, what tune is coming up next. And remember: Corners are lava, stay out of them.

Belonging

A curious staple of UK television, *Come Dine with Me* is a reality show that features a group of strangers competing to throw the best dinner party. Contestants each take turns hosting the others, subjecting their competitors to an evening of food, conversation and entertainment. The guests mark each other out of 10 and the winner gets a cash prize. As with many reality shows, the producers seem to select the contestants with the aim of generating conflict, but a cringe-inducing sense of awkwardness peaks—quite regularly—when a host makes the evening entirely about themselves: "Why wouldn't everyone want to see a slideshow of my niece's graduation?" Or, "Just wait until you see what I learned in my burlesque class."

Take note: Effective entertaining never centers on the host. Think about the social gatherings you've recently enjoyed. Does your mind travel first to the person who orchestrated it? More likely, you think of the feelings they engendered in you—a sense of warmth, relaxation and most importantly, of belonging.

We feel as if we belong when we recognize ourselves in those around us. Alex Law, professor of sociology at Abertay University in Scotland, explains this using 18th-century economist Adam Smith's idea of "moral sympathy." "We routinely try to see ourselves as we imagine others might see us. We know that others are looking at and judging us, and that we are also looking at and judging them," Law says. He quotes Robert Burns' 1786 poem, "To a Louse," to emphasize his point: "O wad some Power the giftie gie us/To see oursels as ithers see us!" This sense of mutually reinforcing commonality is the key to creating group affinity. It also underlies the idea of "collective effervescence": the euphoria you feel when excitement cascades through a crowd, lowering your emotional inhibitions—whether it's at a football game, nightclub, political demonstration or music festival. Sociologist Émile Durkheim first applied this idea to religious gatherings. "People gather to perform sacred devotions wholly separate from the profane world," Law explains. "This allows the group to transcend the usual everyday taboos on self-control and become ecstatic as a collective body. Durkheim argues that they are actually worshipping themselves." So, can secular rituals generate this sense of communal self-worship in a contemporary social setting? In his 1903 essay *The Metropolis and Mental Life*, philosopher Georg Simmel pointed to social games and pastimes, such as fashion and flirting, that give us a sense of escape from the overstimulation of urban life. Recently, hipster leisure venues in cities around the world have been offering darts, table tennis and even "urban ax-throwing." These savvy businesses are capitalizing on our desire to feel connected to others through shared rituals with no purpose. In the home setting, it seems appropriate to welcome people with more simple rituals—a nostalgic song, or a meal that you cook for friends every year.

It's worth remembering, however, that our desire to belong is a driving force behind some of our worse behavior, as well as our best. The feeling that leads you to embrace a stranger on the street when your team wins during the World Cup is the same one driving schoolyard bullies, cult leaders and nationalistic politics. What might you unleash if your dinner party goes a bit too well?

Words by *Debika Ray*

Words by *Pip Usher*

Joan Didion once said that we tell ourselves stories in order to live. From first date stories to the well-practiced dinner party anecdote, stories are ways of forging a connection with others—and having fun while we do it. Kentucky native *Bobette Buster*—an author and storytelling virtuoso whose skills are enlisted by Hollywood heavyweights like Pixar—has built a career on deconstructing this age-old art. She shares advice on how to craft a story with emotional resonance, how to walk the delicate line between sharing and oversharing and how the requirement for a gathering to "entertain" can become a pleasure rather than a burden if the responsibility is shared equally among guests and host.

As a guest, how do you ensure that you're an entertaining addition to a party? It's such a wonderful thing to be invited to gather as a group. As such, I feel that it's a guest's responsibility to give something of themselves—to listen well, and to draw out the others so that everyone feels they were part of the evening. After a party like that, you come away feeling uplifted and light. I think that's because you haven't dominated the gathering, nor have you held back like a wallflower. You've entered in softly and elegantly.

What are your tips for nailing a successful dinner party anecdote? You need to start from a sense memory—it can be visual or taste or hearing—so that the people listening can feel your story. Then they'll automatically think, "Oh I remember when..." and want to tell their own. You've offered ways for the group to take the baton.

When telling a story, how personal should you get in front of people you're meeting for the first time? It's a little odd if you're too vulnerable immediately, but usually, in the warmth of the evening, it's natural that everyone becomes more open. Just remember that it's not the setting for therapy and it's not the setting to vent. Instead, it's about sharing what could be a communal experience that advances the evening.

How do you strike the right balance between being engaging and overpowering the conversation? I start off with the intention of being very open to new people and to new ideas. I'm very interested in the other person, and there's an astonishment that comes when they know that you're really listening. Everyone has a glib response at first, but when you start genuinely listening and leaning in, people will start to give you a whole other side of themselves.

How can a host draw stories out of people? At some of the best dinner parties that I've gone to, the host has—after the initial sharing of cocktails—asked one question of everyone in the room that is answered over the course of dinner. The question can be something like, "Can you remember an art event that created an emotional, transformative reaction?" Sharing a personal question opens up the group in a very beautiful way. You come away feeling like you've had your world view expanded.

Entertainment

HOW TO LEAVE A PARTY —— WORDS BY JUSTIN MYERS
Once the party is down to a third of its peak populace, it's time to go. People won't want you to leave; it reminds them that it's past their bedtime too. "French exits"—slipping out unseen—are frowned upon; instead, try to find the host or pick the most sober and sensible fellow reveler, and say you must leave now as you're up early tomorrow. If they fail to pass this on, the fault becomes the messenger's.

Trust

Hospitality suggests a generosity of spirit and a full-throated welcome. The hospitable soul not only welcomes visitors but celebrates their arrival. They are curious about where the traveler hails from and where they will be going. They must trust the visitor and be trusted by them in turn.

In ancient Greece, *xenia* was the term for this relationship between host and guest and the concept was a cornerstone of the culture. So crucial was xenia to the Greeks that it was the domain of Zeus, the king of the gods—and the protector of strangers. In myths, Zeus zealously watched over how hosts treated guests and how guests showed them gratitude. The Greeks believed that it would of-fend Zeus himself if welcome was denied to a stranger that turned up on your doorstep.

Great wars in ancient literature have occurred when xenia was ig-nored or insulted, as when Paris stole away with Helen and the Tro-jans offered up that horse. When the trust between the guest and the host was violated, the ancient world would erupt in violence. The gods would furiously choose sides. All would be chaos until xe-nia was restored.

Xenia was celebrated, while xe-nophobia was shunned, rejected, or avoided. This wasn't because the ancient Greeks were a utopi-an people; indeed, they conquered nations and enslaved peoples. They called them barbarians and still had the audacity to demand a warm welcome.

Western civilization was built, at least in part, on the Greek con-cept of hospitality and welcome. On the Statue of Liberty in New York, a bronze plaque featuring the poem "The New Colossus" reads: "Give me your tired, your poor, Your huddled masses yearn-ing to breathe free..." Today, how-ever, our world has upended this principle, choosing to codify xeno-phobia—the fear of strangers—in-stead. Immigrants arriving in for-eign lands, especially those most in need of shelter and asylum, are now resented and distrusted.

This isn't true, however, for those with the great fortune to have credit cards, smartphones, powerful passports and round-trip airfare. For these people, the world remains inviting—a play-ground for work, leisure and per-sonal exploration. With a touch of a screen, and for a fee, these trav-elers can find themselves wel-comed into someone's most inti-mate spaces: They will step into a car driven by a stranger; they will lie down in the guest bedroom of an unknown host.

Globally, governments have chosen to calcify the separation of people and culture, and yet individuals can still find trust and an enthusiastic welcome. They just need the means to em-ploy ride-sharing apps, home-swapping services and co-work-ing spaces.

Words by *Neda Semnani*

Comfort

Good food passed generously among friends, energetic conversation, a sense of familiar ease—it's hard to envision anything quite as agreeable. "Eating is comfort," declares Margaret Visser in *The Rituals of Dinner*. But while a casual gathering might seem like a relaxed form of entertaining, those offhand invitations to have a "quick bite" actually come imbued with their own set of strict standards. "Modern manners," Visser says, "increasingly force us to be casual." We act casually because it's expected, and the price of not complying is almost always awkwardness and discomfort. Wear formal dinner dress to a friendly get-together, and you and everyone else will focus on your clothing all evening. Eating is comfort, as long as you meet expectations.

The more stringent manners of other eras served the same ends as they do now; they set a common tone for an evening so diners could focus on the pleasures of the meal, instead of trying to figure out which fork to use. The 18th-century French gourmand, Jean Anthelme Brillat-Savarin, prescribes just four conditions for an enjoyable dinner: "Food at least passable, good wine, agreeable companions, and enough time." In that age of culinary embellishment and rigid social conventions, dinner guests would have been exquisitely mannered and blithely oblivious to the liveried servants swirling around them. But having conformed to the restraints of polite society—by dressing properly, speaking wittily and consistently choosing the correct fork—any

guest could ensure that "both soul and body enjoy an especial well-being," as Brillat-Savarin put it. Three hundred years later, both comportment and cutlery have changed, but Brillat-Savarin's four conditions have not. M. F. K. Fisher, a great cook and one of the 20th century's most prolific and thoughtful food writers, witnessed the transformation. In *The Gastronomical Me*, she recalls how she planned to entertain guests in her tiny first kitchen: "Let them try eating two or three things, I said, so plentiful and so interesting and so well cooked that they will be satisfied. And if they aren't satisfied, let them stay away from our table, and our leisurely comfortable friendship at that table." Fisher expected her guests to dispense with some of their old etiquette, to

relax a bit. Some did so easily, others more reluctantly. Occasionally, disconcerted guests looked in vain for servants, and, feeling "puzzled and hungry," served themselves directly from the kitchen stove. But as they ate and talked and lingered over empty coffee cups and dessert plates, their formal habits loosened and they began to accept a new set of codes.

The evolving rules of etiquette are extensive, complicated and subtle. It might seem a relief that we don't need to worry about the strict formality of dinner jackets and fish knives any more, but the truth is that, as modern manners push us to be more laid-back, we must live up to expectations that are more elusive than before. The cues that help keep us comfortable are countless—but unwritten.

Words by *Alex Anderson*

How do you throw a successful party? Free-flowing drink and a killer playlist must surely come high on the list, but it's the ability to understand and respond to your guests' emotional needs that will transform their evening into something to be enjoyed rather than politely endured. *Amy Alkon*—advice columnist and author of *Unf*ckology: A Field Guide to Living with Guts and Confidence*—believes that understanding human behavior is key to ensuring that each guest feels included within the party. From smoothing over uncomfortable silences to navigating polarized politics, she applies her brand of blunt advice to empathetic hosting.

Should you seat friends together to avoid embarrassing silences? At the root of good manners is empathy. You need to look at your friends and think about which person is totally horrified at a social function. Put them near a friend; it's like having a life preserver to cling to. But there are some people who are extroverts, who love talking to strangers, and they're the ones who will reach out across the table and say, "Who are you? What's your name?"

If someone does struggle in social situations, is it ever kinder to simply not invite them? I always err on the side of inclusiveness. If people are so introverted that it makes them miserable to go to a party, then they can choose to stay home. But it's always nicer to include them at first, and then they can give you a phony excuse.

What's the most considerate way to be a matchmaker for single guests? What you want to do is provide a naturalistic environment. If you think about the Great Plains, gazelles are just grazing there. They'll go, "Oh look, there's some grass, I'll go eat that grass." There aren't handlers pushing them toward those grassy patches. As the host, you want to create an environment where there's ample opportunity for conversation. One way to do that is to have activities—it's a way to get everyone to talk to each other and to laugh and be natural and forget themselves.

Should a host insist on certain topics being off-limits? At dinner parties I think there should be a preparatory conversation to declare a moratorium on politics. If you speak of it, you'll be fined $5 for the host's favorite charity. The goal for the party is to be connecting as people, and seeing one another as co-humans. Look for commonalities with other people in real life and save your fights for Twitter.

When can a host can put aside their guests' needs and prioritize their own? You do not want to be pathologically empathetic. This is where you're not just being kind at a small cost to yourself but when you're incurring a huge cost emotionally or even financially. You don't have to invite people who are not guest-worthy. They should have the bare minimum of socially acceptable behavior: They can't ruin the furniture, shout, get into drunken arguments. You need to be kind to yourself, too.

Empathy

Words by *Pip Usher*

Thank you all for your wishes and gifts, and for your lovely presence too!

HOW TO WRITE A THANK-YOU NOTE — WORDS BY JUSTIN MYERS

In an age of incivility, manners can be seen as quaint, but here's some insider info: There's no greater way to show consideration and gratitude for your host's efforts than by sending a humble thank-you note. Make it personal, sincere and light on schmaltz. Referring to an in-joke, something particular you liked or in the case of a gift, when or how you'll use it, makes it clear you're not hammering these out on a production line.

MR. LARKIN

MRLARKIN.COM

4
Directory

Photograph: Jerome De Perlinghi / Corbis via Getty Images

JOHN CLIFFORD BURNS

John Waters

A conversation with the world's most audacious bad-tastemaker.

Filmmaker John Waters achieved what he calls a "sort-of fame" based on his bad taste and others' bad reviews. "If someone vomits watching one of my films, it's like getting a standing ovation," he once wrote. Sincerely shameless during the 1970s, when the obscenity of movies such as *Pink Flamingos* shocked audiences, Waters seems to have softened into his 70s; the latest role in his filmography was a part in *Alvin and the Chipmunks*. His darkly subversive humor—a lifelong motif—may have long since migrated from the fringes of counterculture into the mainstream, but he, his legacy and his trademark pencil moustache retain cult status. With a retrospective of his visual art opening at the Baltimore Museum of Art, Waters—whose genteel manner belies his proclivity for shocking audiences—explains the visceral nature of art, how he has responded to societal shifts over the decades and the fun in failure.

If art is therapy, what sort does your work encourage? I believe in therapy; I always buy the Kleenex boxes they sell at the Freud Museum gift shop. If my artwork is therapy in any way, it's probably through making you laugh—in a good way, at something that you love. I'm taking the neurosis, the joy and the horror that comes from the art world and the movie business and trying to celebrate it. I'm making fun of insider knowledge, but I love that insider knowledge.

And which artworks have you found most formative? When I was a kid, I first saw Duchamp's *Nude Descending a Staircase* in *Life* magazine and I pretended I was that painting every day; apparently, I did very peculiar walks when I came down the stairs. The first artwork I ever bought—I think it cost a dollar—was a little [Gustave] Moreau poster in the Baltimore Museum. I took it home and the other kids were like, "Eww, it's ugly. Why would you have that?" And then I realized the power of art that could make people crazy and angry, so right then, I became a collector. People hate all art when it first comes out because it destroys what came before.

Was that your intention? Your own work is renowned for its shock value. I used to get fined for obscenity all the time. I would see my movies screen at midnight and see what joyous occasions they were, but then I would go into the courtroom at 9 a.m. and have to watch them again and it was really obscene. So it's all about perception and the when and where.

Is it easier to shock people in a gallery or in a movie theater? I'm never just trying to shock people—that was 50 years ago when there was a society that *could* be shocked. Hollywood now makes $100 million out of gross comedies that aren't funny. I still try to make you laugh. There are certain works now that are probably just as rude as anything I've ever done, but I think people understand it a little more and times have changed a lot. I don't think you could walk through my show and think that I've made some phony attempt to get respectable. I have a piece called *Twelve Assholes and a Dirty Foot*, but it comes with a beautiful velvet curtain that you can close if, let's say, your parents are coming over or the IRS is auditing you and coming to your house. Sometimes you have to hide your art.

How does it feel to have a new retrospective in your beloved Baltimore? The Baltimore Museum was the first place that my films were shown with taxpayer money when I was definitely not cinematically correct; they had a whole series of my movies and got some hassle about it. I think it will be a great homecoming: You very much want to be in a museum where you grew up, where you first saw contemporary art and where you still live.

Your work has always celebrated failure. How do you deal with your own shortcomings? You never know what's going to work or what's going to fail. I've been doing this for 50 years. I've had movies that were failures, I've had movies that were hits. It makes me nervous whenever anybody I'm working on a project with says, "This is going to be great!" It's like a curse. Don't count your blessings before it happens.

My early career was built on bad reviews, but the right kind of bad reviews. There was a cultural war, and the critics didn't get that a bad review could help. I can't imagine the right kind of a bad review I could get now. Of course, there is still a cultural war going on... I always try to think about what art Trump would have in his apartment. I mean, some of Jeff Koons' early work might look great in there, but he wouldn't see the irony.

Waters' moustache is fashioned after that of musician Little Richard, a childhood idol whose songs appear in several of his movies.

HOT POCKETS
by Harriet Fitch Little

Jeans can look silly: Fake rips and applied bleach stains have made a design famed for its practicality feel anything but. Don't mistake the tiny inner pocket on the front right of jeans for just another embellishment, however. Introduced by the father of modern denim, Levi Strauss, the pocket was added to blue jeans around the 1870s so that miners in Gold Rush-era California could protect their precious pocket watches from getting crushed on the job. Later, the practical appeal of that safe pouch contributed to cowboys' (now iconic) affection for Levi's. (Top: iPhone cover from Building Block. Center: Chalk Shelby Bucket Bag by Filippa K. Bottom: Gallery Accessories Buckle Bag by Ganni.)

KATIE CALAUTTI

Object Matters

A short history of pockets—and why women lack them.

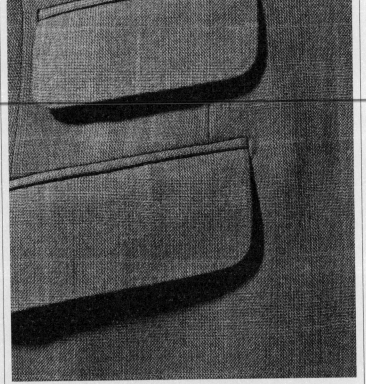

What's in your pockets? If the answer is, "I don't have any," then you're probably wearing a garment designed for women. The fist-sized pouch of hidden fabric holds a surprisingly gendered history.

In 1250 A.D. in medieval England, both men and women strapped bags to the outside of their tunics. As fashions changed, fitchets—slits in outerwear that allowed access to bags worn hidden beneath—became au courant.

A few hundred years later in the 17th century, men's fashion took a giant leap forward in functionality: Slimmer versions of purses were sewn into the seams of breeches to deter thieves. In the 1800s, tailors standardized a suit design still used today, featuring 17 pockets that could hold any number of necessities. A figure thusly outfitted was someone to reckon with: a man with as many means as he had space to store them.

Women's clothing, on the other hand, continued to offer inconvenient or nonexistent places for valuables. Accessing under-garment bags was a complicated endeavor, and when the 1700s ushered in slimmer Grecian-inspired fashions with no room to hide bulky pouches, storage was removed altogether and resigned to handheld purses. By the 1800s, it was clear that pockets symbolized two things: power and privacy—freedoms females were not granted. It was assumed that women had nothing of value to hold, and no agency to hold it.

To this day, women lack convenient garment storage. Major strides were made in the early 1900s when women co-opted menswear and donned pants. But the 1950s ushered in a revival of slimmed-down designs, with little room for hip-exaggerating pockets. In 1954, Christian Dior reportedly said, "Men have pockets to keep things in, women for decoration."

Blame it on sexism in the fashion industry (and beyond), or the commercialism of the handbag industry, but for such a seemingly small feat of design, the weight of your pockets isn't just determined by what's inside them.

Left Photographs: Courtesy of Building Block (Top), Filippa K (Middle), Ganni (Bottom), Right Photograph: Aaron Tilley, Jacket: Charlie Allen Bespoke

Writer and former dancer *Suzanne Snider* remembers *Isadora Duncan*: the rebel dancer who challenged classical ballet more than a century ago.

SUZANNE SNIDER

Peer Review

Duncan is known as the mother of modern expressive dance. "The dancer of the future will dance, not in the form of nymph, nor fairy, nor coquette, but in the form of woman in its greatest and purest expression," she once wrote.

Photography: Elvira Studio / Bibliothèque de l'Opera Garnier / Archives Charmet / Bridgeman Images

Last May, inside a small recital hall, I watched as 10 dancers under the age of six balanced tall peacock feathers in their palms. They wore pink silk tunics and flowers in their hair (the sole boy in the group wore green) to celebrate 16 weeks of training as "Duncan dancers." How I landed at this recital involved four years of parenting (my daughter was among the performers) and more than a century of Isadora Duncan's artistic influence on the world.

Duncan is often described as the mother of modern dance, a legacy eclipsed by the more sensational details of her personal life. For the young Duncan dancers on stage, it mattered little that Duncan, born in 1877, had been—among other things—bisexual, an atheist and a communist sympathizer, or that she adopted six of her female dance students (popularly referred to as "The Isadorables"). My daughter doesn't know that Duncan gave birth to three children by three different fathers (two children drowned and the third died shortly after birth) or of Duncan's storied death by strangulation when her long silk scarf became trapped in a wheel of a moving car. (This final tragedy inspired Gertrude Stein's quip, "Affectation can be dangerous.") All of this is of lesser importance to dance historians, as well, who

cite Duncan's break from ballet as her major contribution. Duncan campaigned for "natural" movement, which involved bare feet, sheer and flowy toga-like clothing and stripped-down sets; a Duncan dancer's movement and energy comes from her solar plexus, a radical departure from the rigidity of the balletic torso.

This made little impression on me as a student of dance in the 1990s; Duncan felt less like our mother and more like an embarrassing great aunt—overly emotional and a little old-fashioned. I rejected nature as source material. I realize now that her coup was too successful for us to notice there had been a coup at all. Her return to walking, skipping and breathing as dance had paved the way for the "pedestrian" and "gestural" work by postmodern choreographers whose work I found more edgy and cool.

Dance critic Deborah Jowitt described Duncan's technique as a form "that expressed woman's freedom... to put away corsets, take lovers, bear children out of wedlock, and to dance like that kind of woman..." How had I missed this transmission of radical feminism? My daughter and the rest of the 2018 cohort of Duncan dancers were wiser; they eagerly received and embodied this offering and I now understood it as liberation.

Cult Rooms

Galerie Maeght: The shape-shifting gallery where the greatest generation of French artists got its start.

Rue du Bac, in Paris' aristocratic seventh arrondissement, has always been an artistic address. Salonist Madame de Staël once lived at number 97. The American painter Whistler resided, without his mother, at number 110. And number 120 was home to François-René de Chateaubriand, a writer who had a cut of steak named after him. It's that sort of *rue*.

If they were alive today, de Staël, Whistler and Chateaubriand would surely frequent Galerie Maeght at number 42. Its double vitrine tells the tale of how a lowly lithographer from the south of France, Aimé Maeght, rose to become one of the most powerful players in the modern art world. Postcards and exhibition posters speak of previous shows by César, Marc Chagall and Alexander Calder. And that's just the Cs.

The Aimé Maeght legend starts in France's deep south back in 1930. The likes of Pablo Picasso, Henri Matisse and Raoul Dufy had all moved to the sun-kissed strip between Cannes and Nice. One morning, the elderly post-impressionist Pierre Bonnard rushed into Maeght's shop and ordered the printing of a concert program that featured one of his works. The copy sold immediately, prompting Bonnard to contribute another work, and another. Maeght's method of reproducing lithographed art for the masses, at a lower cost than an original canvas, would go on to help democratize contemporary visual culture.

War did not halt Maeght's ambition. As France capitulated to Nazi Germany in 1940, art became a currency in itself. The young printer would sneak up to occupied Paris and snag canvases from Bonnard's studio. Then he would paint a slapdash scene in soluble watercolor to hide the priceless layer below, which could be washed off on safe return to the south. In this manner, Maeght provided wartime sustenance to what was perhaps France's greatest generation of artists.

In 1945, thousands of artists decamped from cities still under fire during the war to Paris, where Maeght had snapped up a gallery for a song. When Matisse wanted to sell his entire wartime production, he turned to his former neighbor and friend from the south. La Galerie Maeght (which started on rue de Téhéran before moving to rue du Bac) could afford to take a chance on up-and-coming artists, including Alberto Giacometti, then a little-known Swiss sculptor and painter, and a young Francis Bacon.

Maeght blurred the lines between publisher, lithographer and art dealer. "With more than one-and-a-half million apartments a year being constructed in Europe… I got the idea that great painters should do limited series of lithos so the greatest number of people could buy it," he once explained.

The Galerie Maeght legend was burnished with iconic exhibitions. Poorer customers snapped up the gallery's inventive show posters, which were a novelty at the time: A 1958 poster advertising American hard-line minimalist Ellsworth Kelly showed a simple white-on-black "X." Underneath were typed the words Galerie Maeght, with no address or telephone number needed.

Maeght's next big idea was born out of sorrow. After the death of his son Bernard in 1953, Maeght sailed to New York to see the Guggenheim and Barnes foundations, both pioneering private art for all. Georges Braque suggested he create something that would "live after" him, Maeght would later recall. The idea was a museum near Nice, where 20th-century artists could show their work in optimum conditions. Fernand Léger said: "If you do that I would even paint the rocks." And so the Fondation Maeght was born. Designed by zany Catalan Josep Lluís Sert, it was the first private museum of its kind in France.

On its opening day in 1964, a rainbow of mobiles by Calder arched over the foundation entrance. Entire spaces were designed in close collaboration with artists, like Braque's mammoth mosaic pool known as *Les Poissons*.

The 13,000-piece art space, still thriving today, mirrors Aimé Maeght's original raison d'être: He paired the commercialism of his Parisian gallery with the collaborative culture of the South, then drenched it in year-round sunshine for the entire world to see.

Aimé Maeght was also the founding editor of French art magazine *Derrière le miroir*, which he published for almost 40 years until his death in 1981.

Photograph: Christian Møller Andersen

GALERIE MAEGHT

42

ALEX ANDERSON

Closer Encounters

What should we say to aliens?

Humankind is listening for messages from space, waiting to hear from the intelligent beings that must be out there—somewhere. The SETI Institute's search for extraterrestrial intelligence directs massive telescope arrays and countless citizen-scientists to sift through the hum of the cosmos for some meaningful irregularity.

In 1977, the Voyager Golden Record was sent into orbit on both of the Voyager spacecraft. Featuring Chuck Berry's "Johnny B. Goode," whale song and greetings in 55 languages, it was a hodgepodge of hellos intended for alien ears. But those were simpler times. The question of whether we should intentionally convey messages to space beings has become a fraught question. In 2015, a large group of scientists concurred that because we have no idea how extraterrestrials might react, "a worldwide scientific, political and humanitarian discussion must occur before any message is sent." This seems wise.

If we did try to communicate with aliens today, how would we do it, and what would we say? First, we may want to practice on creatures closer to home. Dogs understand a few words and respond nicely to treats, so that's a start. Octopuses, philosopher Peter Godfrey-Smith contends, are "probably the closest we will come to meeting an intelligent alien." They commu-

nicate with variations in skin color and texture, and, understanding three-dimensional arrangements, can recognize individual human faces. So in order to connect with an octopus, we might use shifting patterns or facial expressions. Octopus intelligence is so different from ours, however, that it's hard to imagine what they might find meaningful, besides treats—which they also like.

Canines and cephalopods demonstrate that if we want to get in touch with extraterrestrials, it would help to know something about them—what they look like, how they communicate, how they think. We don't have this advantage, so we have to assume they'd be smart enough to interpret whatever we have to say.

That was the assumption that guided the Voyager missions 41 years ago. According to NASA, each spacecraft is now 13 billion miles from Earth, carrying "a greeting to any form of life, should that be encountered." An alien playing a Golden Record would find images of people and places along with ideas and greetings. Most of these say something like, "Hello everybody," or "Peace," but the most welcoming exclaims: "Friends of space, how are you all? Have you eaten yet? Come visit us if you have time." After all, we know from experience that most beings respond well to treats.

TOY STORY

by Harriet Fitch Little

Within days, a once-diversely occupied group of children may be found absorbed in an identical activity: playing marbles, trading Pokémon cards or twirling fidget spinners. Adults can only look at the latest obsession with bemusement—or ban it. Observed more closely, however, playground crazes aren't so strange. They're simply an extreme example of the human urge to covet our neighbor's anything—an impulse made more potent for children by the peer pressure of a fenced-in space and the fact that, unlike your neighbor's car, sprinkler system or voice-activated alarm—toys are generally more affordable. (Top: Duotone Car No2 by Ikonic Toys. Center: Playing cards by HAY. Bottom: Natural stacker by Wooden Story.)

Left Photograph: NASA / Getty Images. Right Photographs: Courtesy of WallpaperSTORE* (Top, Middle), Wooden Story (Bottom)

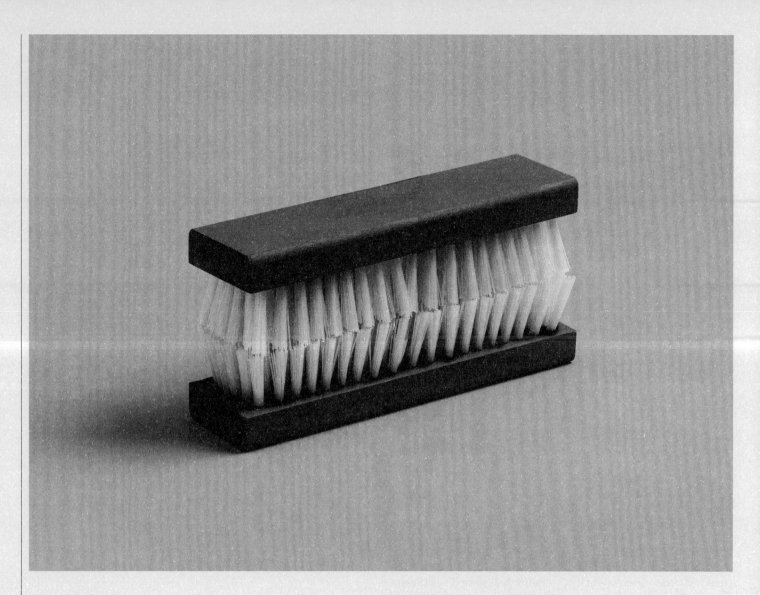

Photograph: Justin Poulsen / The Licensing Project

JOHN OVANS

Inside Out

A joke shared is a joke halved.

Alfred Hitchcock's cameo appearances in his own movies became such a popular in-joke that he eventually started scheduling them for within the first 30 minutes so as not to distract audiences from the main plot.

Inside jokes work differently than most forms of humor. It doesn't matter if other people don't find them funny; that's not the point. In fact, they retain power precisely because other people don't get them.

Done right, they can recall years of shared experiences, and therefore are rich in emotional currency. You and another, or others, become—even if only briefly—members of an exclusive club. To better understand the inside joke's functioning, consider what happens when they fail: On *The Office*, hapless boss Michael Scott's desperate winks and attempts at shared references are almost universally met with silent, stony faces. "I love inside jokes. I'd love to be a part of one someday," he says, grinning maniacally. The problem for Scott is that his club is one that nobody wants to join. Beyond friendships, inside jokes exist wherever community does. TV showrunners regularly forge bonds with fans via cheeky insertions: After discovering there was a drinking game where players had to take a shot every time character Jack Bauer shouted "dammit!" on *24*, actor Kiefer Sutherland decided to ad-lib 14 extra "dammits" in a single episode.

The internet has allowed private gags to go global via GIFs, hashtags and memes—dubbed "the inside jokes of the internet." Often, however, this kind of viral humor begins to work independently of its origins, and the inside joke dies. Once enjoyed by people other than the intended audience, it becomes an outside joke. Inclusion, it seems, just isn't as funny.

Cocktail arithmetic: Mix the clued ingredients together and create classic drinks.

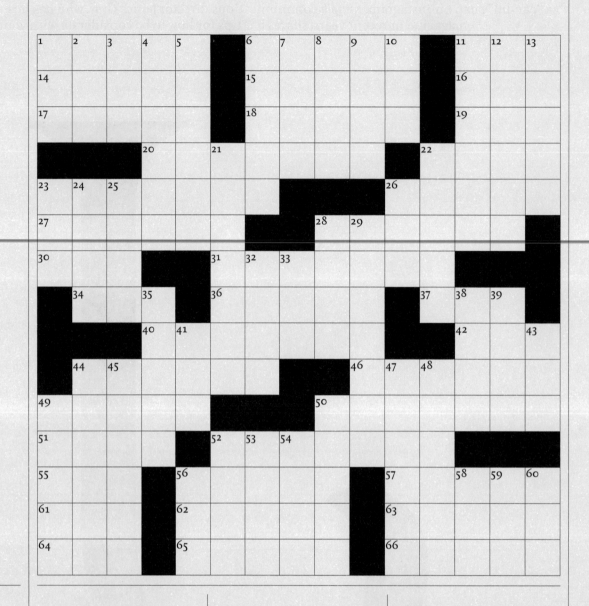

MOLLY YOUNG

Crossword

ACROSS

1. 1 Across + 6 Across + 11 Across + Champagne =French 75
6. 6 Across + 11 Across + 1 Across + 25 Down= Tom Collins
11. 11 Across + Campari + sweet vermouth = Negroni
14. Delete
15. Sheeplike
16. Historical period
17. New York's ___Island
18. "*Our Lady of the Flowers*" author
19. Delivery person?
20. Outlines
22. Eat
23. Poison that appears in Agatha Christie mysteries
26. Possessed
27. Improves
28. Frightened
30. Fish commonly used in fish sticks
31. Toto from "*The Wizard of Oz*," eg.
34. Cultural Revolution leader Zedong
36. Animal life
37. Old-fashioned watch chain
40. 40 Across + 1 Across + 6 Across = Whiskey Sour
42. Rotten
44. Anonymous internet meanies
46. "*Risky Business*" actor Tom
49. Drew back, like a timid horse
50. Type in again, as a password
51. Male cats
52. Cartographical books
55. 55 Across + Coca Cola = Cuba Libre
56. Trojan War epic
57. Instrument played by Yo-Yo Ma
61. Go gray, perhaps
62. 62 Across + grapefruit juice = Greyhound
63. Privileged group
64. Advanced academic degree, for short
65. Guide
66. 66 Across + 11 Across + dry vermouth = Martini

DOWN

1. Spot
2. Web address
3. Guy's counterpart
4. Parenthetical comments
5. Begrudge
6. Sound reasoning
7. Balanced
8. Source of gold or diamonds
9. Small bills
10. Tool for catching fish or butterflies
11. Twin Zodiac sign
12. Decreased?
13. Identified
21. "*A ___ of Dollars*" (1964 Spaghetti Western with Clint Eastwood)
22. Friend of Snow White
23. The Jackson 5 hit
24. Study or kitchen, for example
25. 25 Down + 1 Across + 55 Across + mint + lime = Mojito
26. Raw mineral
28. River under the Ponte Vecchio
29. Grooms-to-be
32. Notable elephant feature
33. Massage
35. Woodwind instruments
38. Memorial newspaper notice
39. Acid neutralizer
41. Antiquated
43. Architect Mies van ___ Rohe
44. Nevertheless
45. Horn-____ glasses
47. Reverberate again
48. Open, as a letter
49. Bra component
50. Navigation aid
52. Heaps and heaps
53. Blondie's "The ___ Is High"
54. "Loch" in English
56. Hospital drips, for short
58. 56, to Ovid
59. "*My Name Is Asher ___*" (Chaim Potok novel)
60. Sugary suffix

The presence of an overzealous photographer often makes an intimate gathering feel like the exact opposite. Food goes cold, and friends can start to feel like props: It's hard to relax when your every gesture might end up in a "candid" snap on Instagram. *Kinfolk* communications director *Jessica Gray*, who has hosted many events for the magazine in recent years, shares her tips for how to be considerate with your camera.

J

I feel strongly that, in our digital age, being invited over to someone's home to spend time with them should be savored. I'd never regret taking photos of the people I love and the great times we've had together, but it irks me when I feel a guest is spending time and energy trying to get the perfect photo throughout the entire evening. There's a balance to strike. Personally, I'm not one to take photos of my food, but I have friends who simply love food and food styling, and will always snap a quick photo. If you must, best to be brief. Don't change the lighting or move things around the table to compose a shot, unless it's explicit among the whole group that now is the time for a photo. I remember being at a friend's house for dinner, and when he brought out the main course it was an absolutely stunning spread—like a Renaissance still life painting. We all quickly stood up to take a photo of the bounty and then put our phones away to enjoy the meal together. I don't have any hard rules per se, but if I take a photo at a friend's house I will usually ask if it's okay if I post it to a public audience before sharing. And keep in mind that there are many ways to remember a gathering: Taking a photo of the table mess at the end of the night can be a brilliant way to record an evening while also allowing you to give your phone some time off during the actual meal.

Tina Frey Designs
tinafreydesigns.com

tf

Stockists

AGENT PROVOCATEUR
agentprovocateur.com

AGNONA
agnona.com

ALLEN EDMONDS
allenedmonds.com

ANDERSON & SHEPPARD
anderson-sheppard.co.uk

A.P.C.
apc.fr

ATELIER SWAROVSKI
atelierswarovski.com

BILLY REID
billyreid.com

BRIONI
brioni.com

BROOKLYN TAILORS
brooklyn-tailors.com

BROOKS BROTHERS
brooksbrothers.com

BUILDING BLOCK
building--block.com

CAUSSE
causse-gantier.fr

CHANEL
chanel.com

CHARLIE ALLEN BESPOKE
charlieallen.co.uk

CHARVET
charvet.com

CORNELIANI
corneliani.com

COS
cosstores.com

DAKS
daks.com

DE FURSAC
defursac.fr

DEREK LAM 10 CROSBY
dereklam.com

DIOR
dior.com

EDIE PARKER
edie-parker.com

FALKE
falke.com

FILIPPA K
filippa-k.com

FRAMA
framacph.com

GANNI
ganni.com

GENERAL EYEWEAR
generaleyewear.com

GIANVITO ROSSI
gianvitorossi.com

HAKUI
hakui-shop.com

HAY
hay.dk

HELMUT LANG
helmutlang.com

HERMÈS
hermes.com

IRWIN GARDEN
irwingarden.com

ISOTONER
isotoner.com

JW ANDERSON
j-w-anderson.com

J.M. WESTON
jmweston.com

KVADRAT
kvadrat.dk

LABOUR AND WAIT
labourandwait.co.uk

LAURENCE BOSSION
laurencebossion.com

LOEWE
loewe.com

LOUIS VUITTON
louisvuitton.com

MAISON MARGIELA
maisonmargiela.com

MAISON MICHEL
michel-paris.com

MARC JACOBS
marcjacobs.com

MARK CROSS
markcross.com

MARQUES'ALMEIDA
marquesalmeida.com

MATICEVSKI
tonimaticevski.com

MERCEDES CASTILLO
mercedescastillo.com

MR P.
mrporter.com

MULBERRY
mulberry.com

NEIL BARRETT
neilbarrett.com

PAUL SMITH
paulsmith.com

RAPHAELE CANOT
raphaelecanot.com

ROCHAS
rochas.com

RYAN LO
ryanlo.co.uk

SANDRO
sandro-paris.com

SHUSHU/TONG
shushutongstudio.com

THE ROW
therow.com

TODD SNYDER
toddsnyder.com

WALLPAPERSTORE*
store.wallpaper.com

Credits

COVER
Photographer
Luc Braquet
Stylist
Camille-Joséphine Teisseire
Assistant Stylist
Céline Gaulhiac
Hair
Taan Doan
Makeup
Cyril Laine
Model
Suzie Bird at Elite Paris
Location
Hotel Plaza Athénée, Paris

Suzie wears a dress by Dior, hat by Maison Michel, earrings by Raphaele Canot on White Bird and gloves by Isotoner.

P. 28
Words
Pip Usher

P. 34
Hair & Makeup
Lucy Gibson

P. 37
Retouching
Matilda Persson at La Machine

P. 38 - 39
Images courtesy of Howard Greenberg Gallery

P. 44 - 55
Hair & Makeup
Ashleigh B. Ciucci

P.66 - 79
Set Design
Lianna Fowler
Hair
Rebecca Chang
Makeup
Liz Daxauer at Caren using Bobbi Brown
Casting
Sarah Bunter
Model
Bibi Abdulkadir at Storm Management
Model
Malik Al Jerrari at Supa Model Management
Assistants
Harry Serjan
Benjamin Whitley

P. 150 - 165
Assistant Stylist
Céline Gaulhiac
Hair
Taan Doan
Makeup
Cyril Laine
Model
Alexis Petit at Elite Paris
Model
Suzie Bird at Elite Paris
Location
Hotel Plaza Athénée, Paris

P. 166 - 175
Retouching
Matilda Persson at La Machine

Special Thanks:
Hotel Plaza Athénée
Kenza Oweiss